FOR ORGANS, PIANOS & ELECTRONIC KEYBOARDS

E-Z PLAY TODAY 186

POP & ROCK SONG CLASSICS

E-Z Play TODAY chord notation is designed for playing **standard chord positions** or **single key chords** on all **major brand organs** and **portable keyboards**.

Contents

T0045414

ISBN 978-0-7935-2451-8

HAL•LEONARD® CORPORATION

7777 W. BLUEMOUND RD. P.O. BOX 13819 MILWAUKEE, WI 53213

Anticipation

Registration 4
Rhythm: Rock or Jazz Rock

Words and Music by Carly Simon

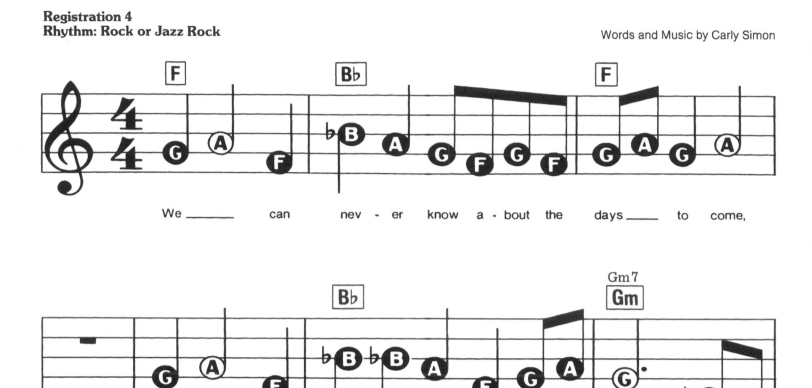

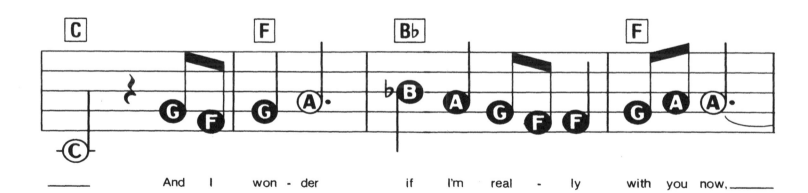

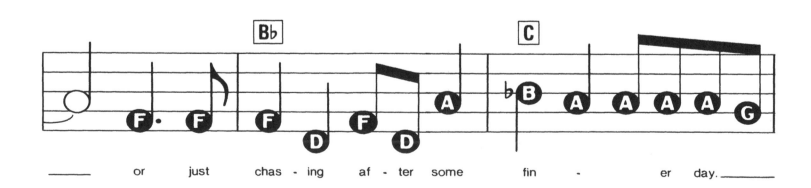

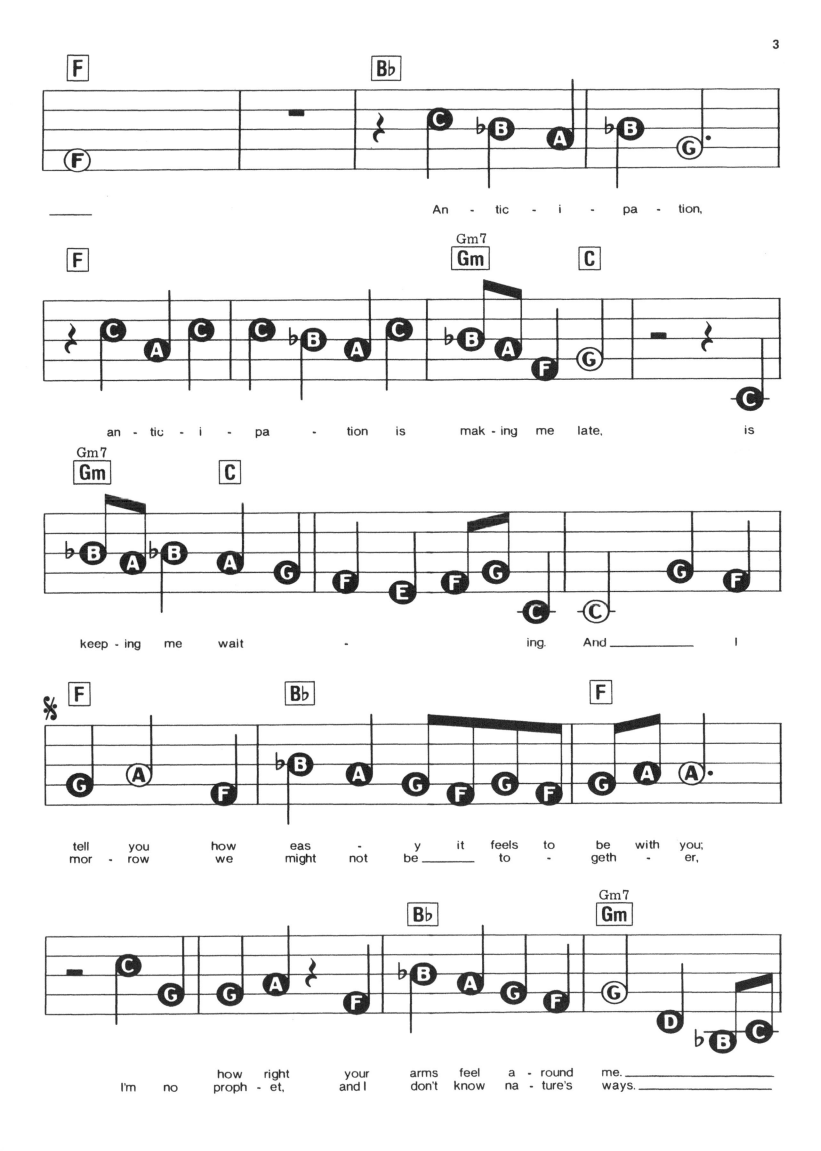

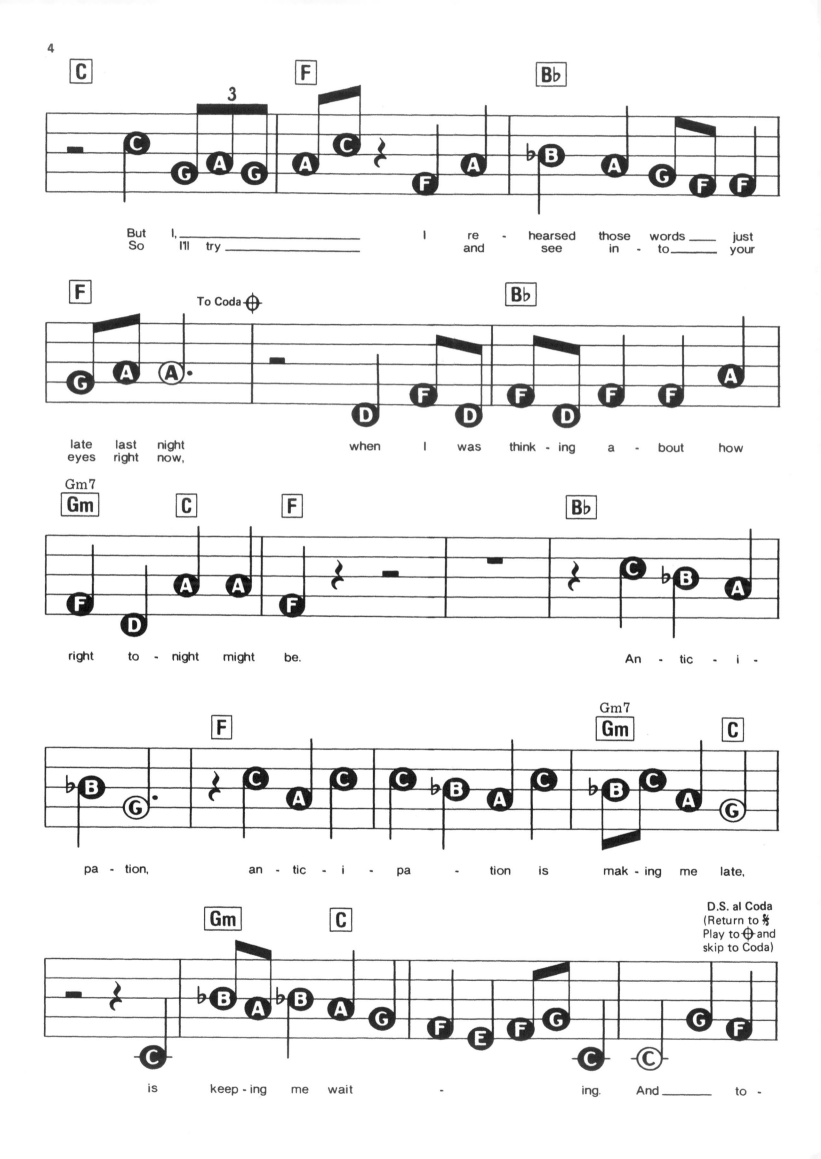

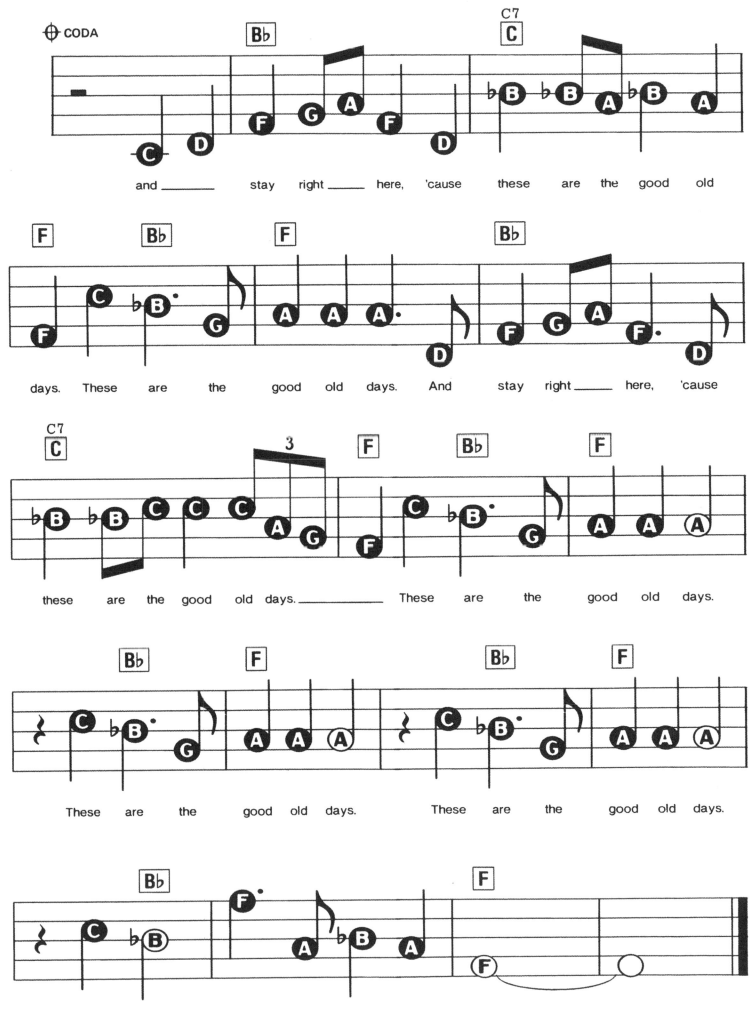

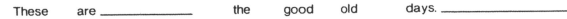

Baby, I'm-A Want You

Registration 4
Rhythm: Slow Rock or Ballad

Words and Music by David Gates

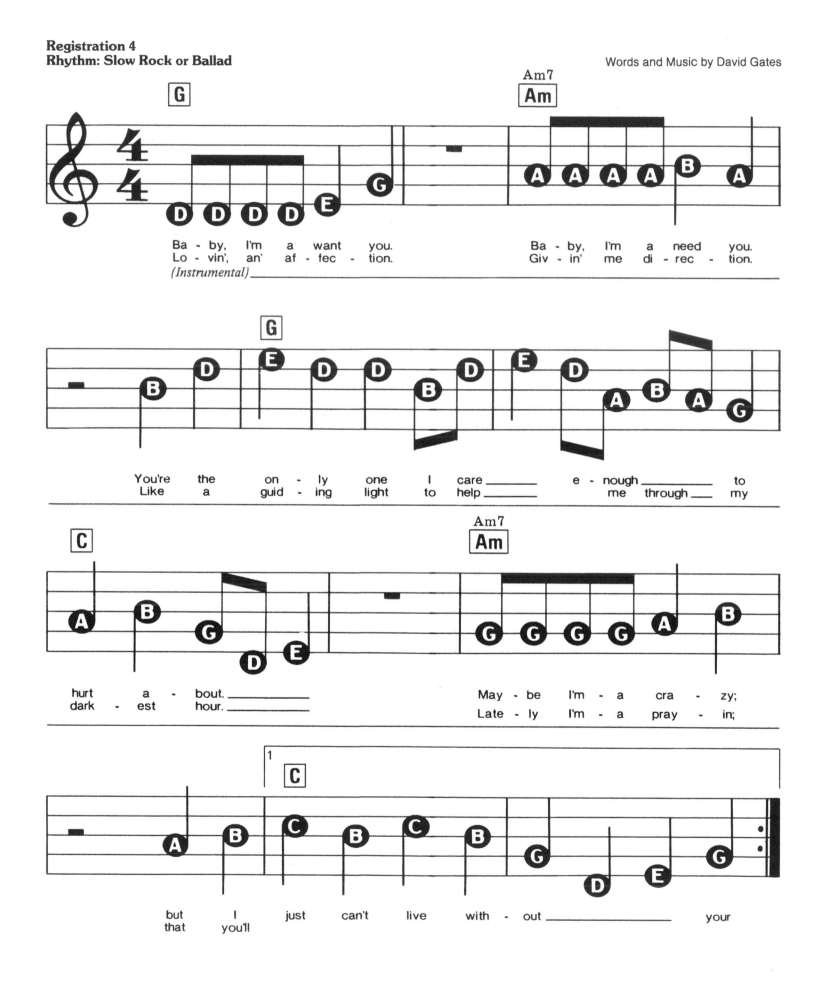

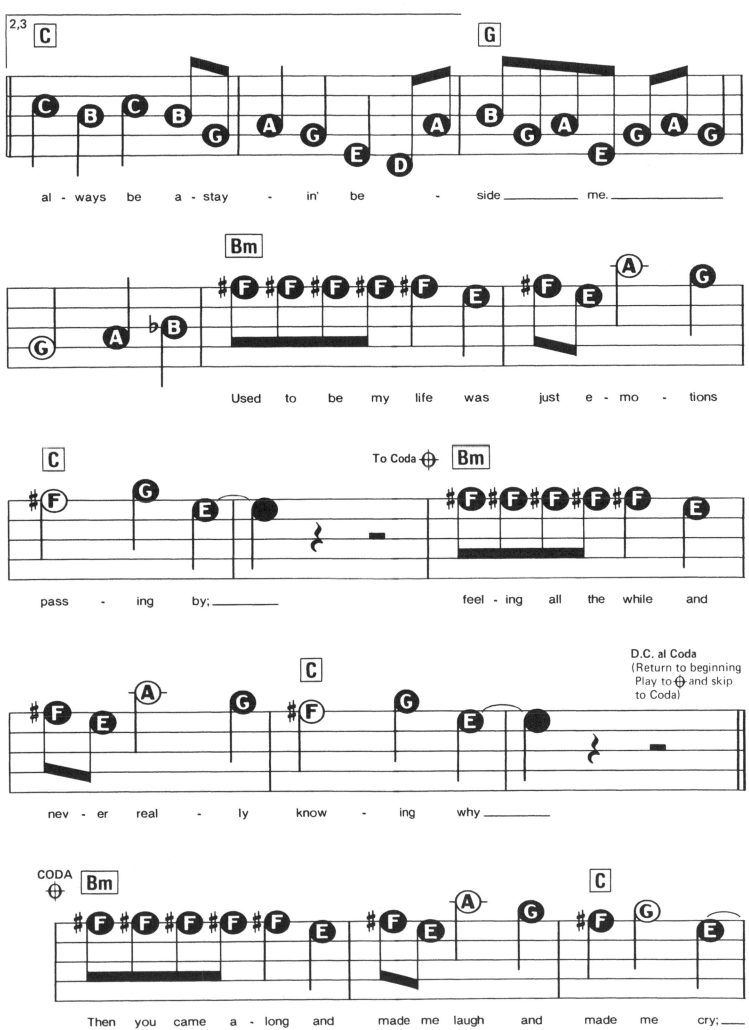

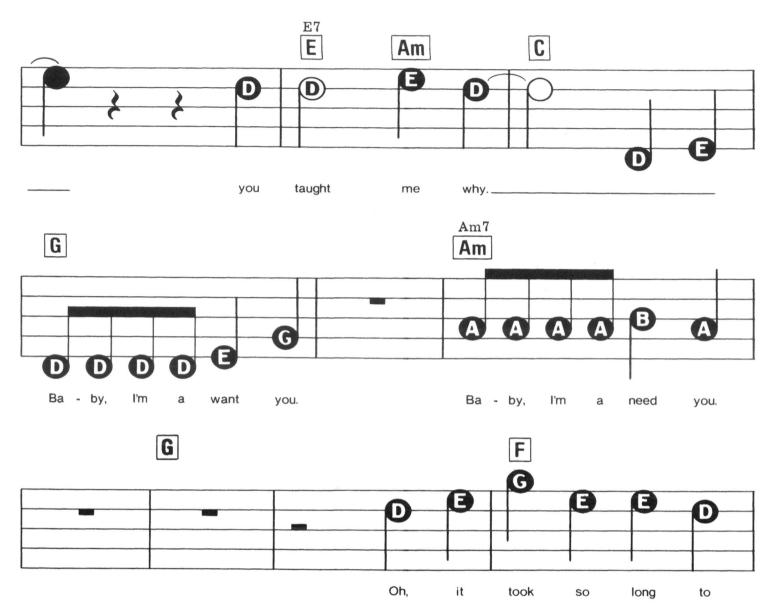

you taught me why. _____

Ba - by, I'm a want you.

Ba - by, I'm a need you.

Oh, it took so long to

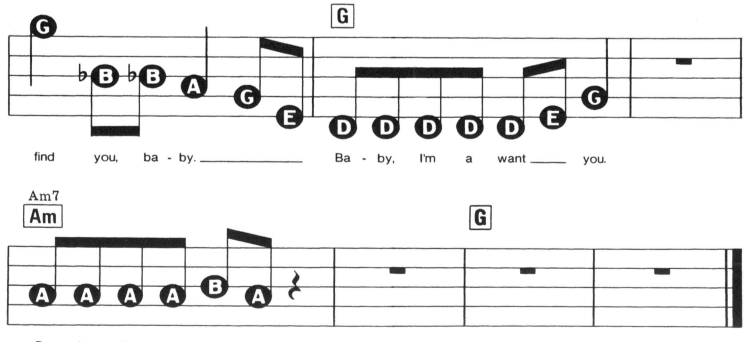

find you, ba - by. _____ Ba - by, I'm a want _____ you.

Ba - by, I'm - a need you.

Goodbye Girl

(From the MGM-Warner Bros. Release of the Neil Simon Production "THE GOODBYE GIRL")

Registration 2
Rhythm: Slow Rock or Ballad

Words and Music by David Gates

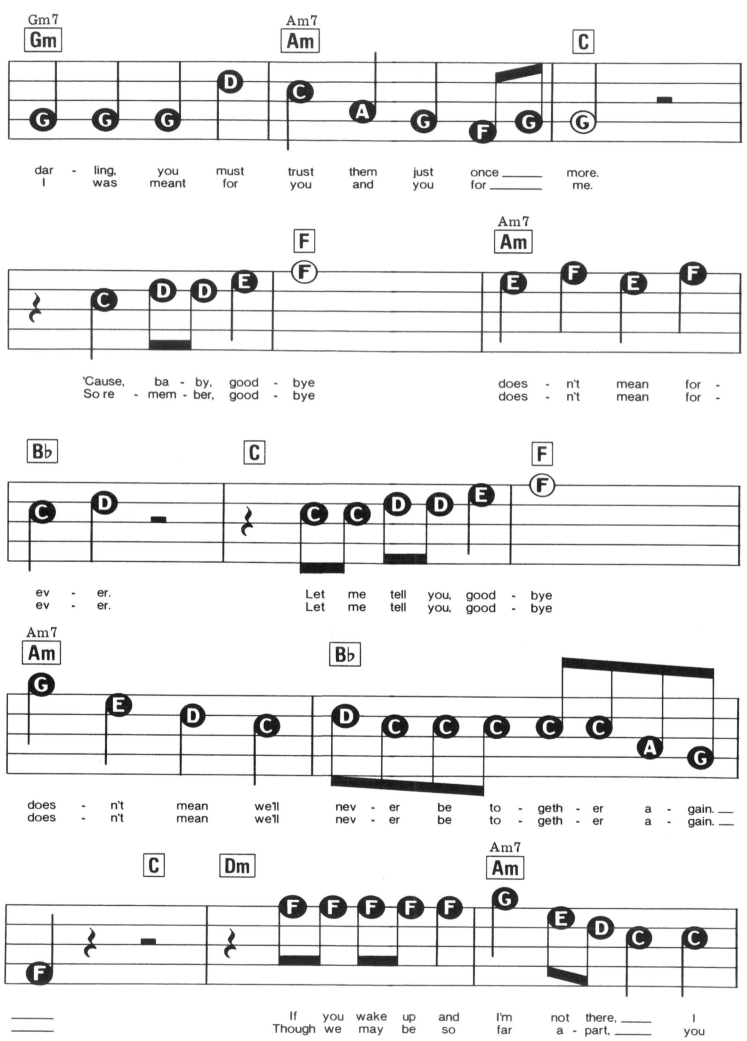

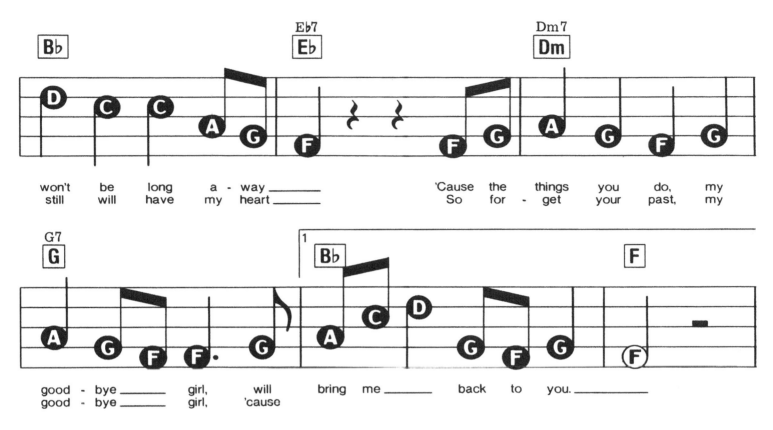

won't   be   long   a - way _____   'Cause   the   things   you   do,   my
still   will   have   my   heart _____   So   for - get   your   past,   my

good - bye _____ girl,   will   bring   me _____ back   to   you. _____
good - bye _____ girl,   'cause

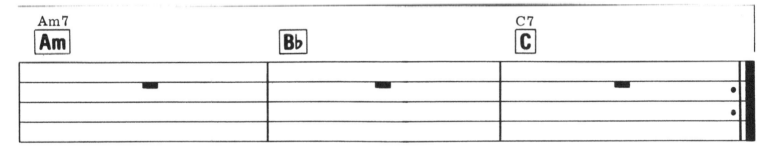

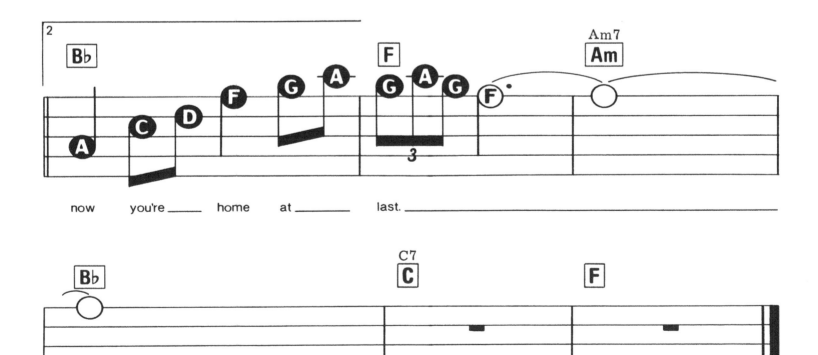

now   you're _____ home   at _____ last. _____

The Best Of My Love

Registration 9
Rhythm: Rock or Disco

Words and Music by Don Henley,
Glenn Frey & John David Souther

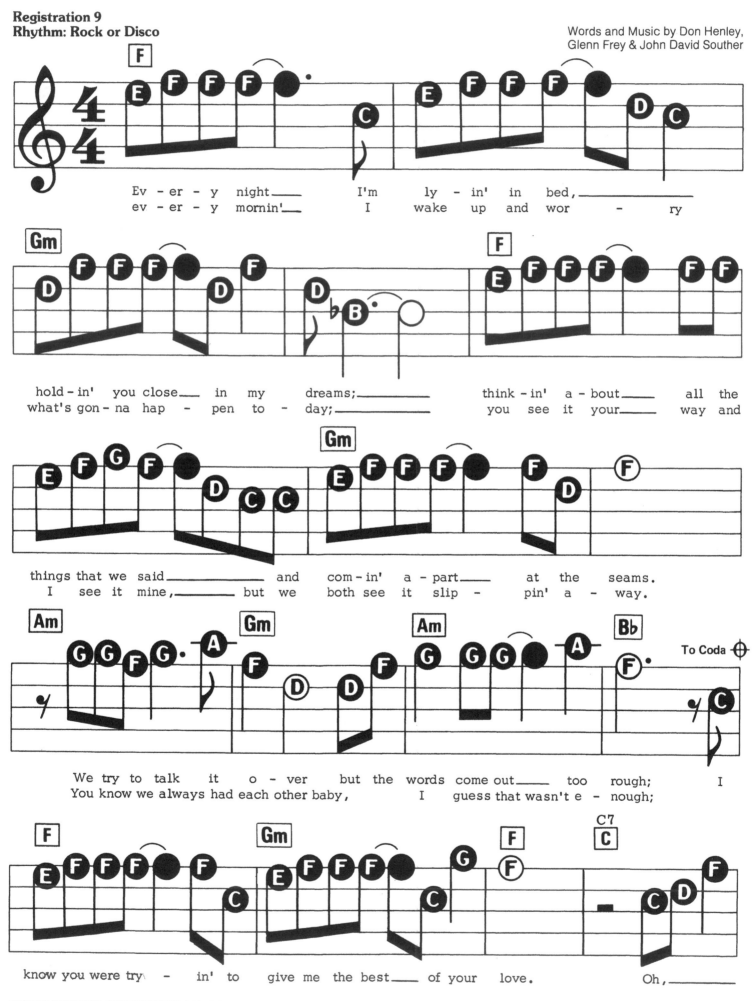

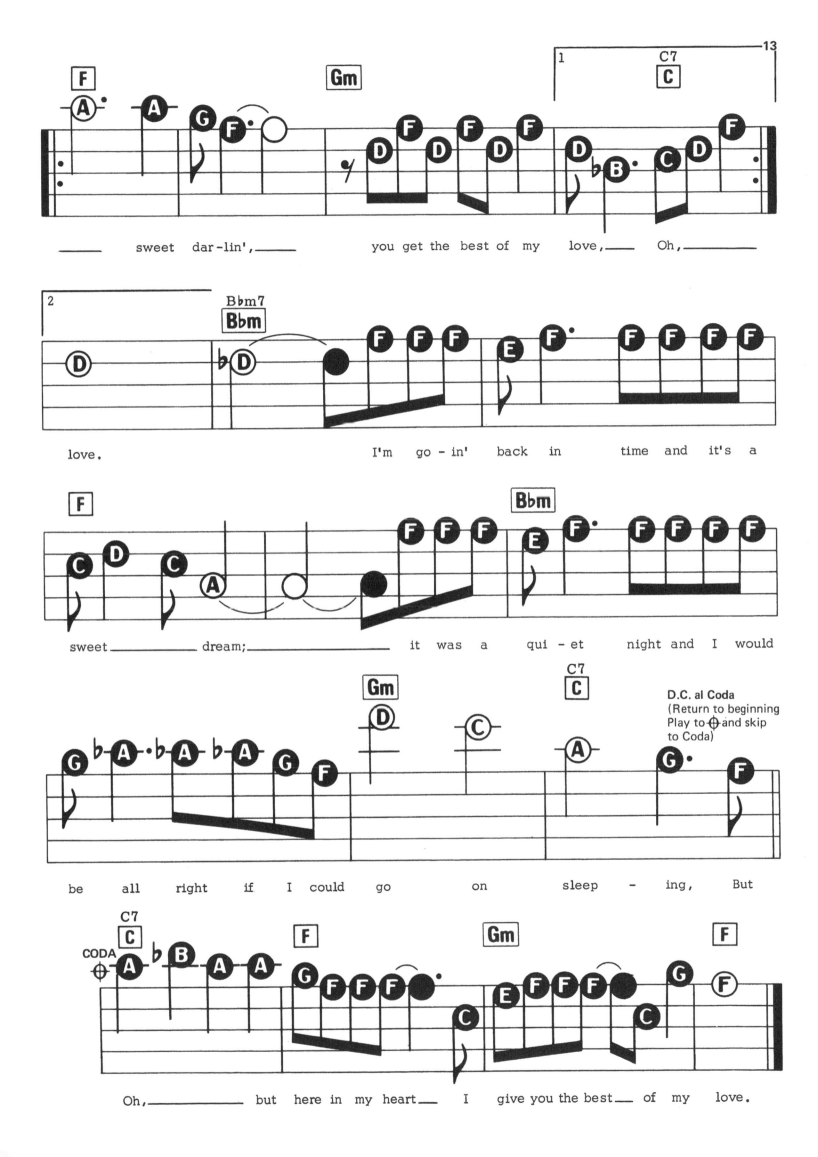

Bless The Beasts And Children

Registration 3
Rhythm: Slow Rock or Ballad

Words and Music by Barry DeVorzon
and Perry Botkin, Jr.

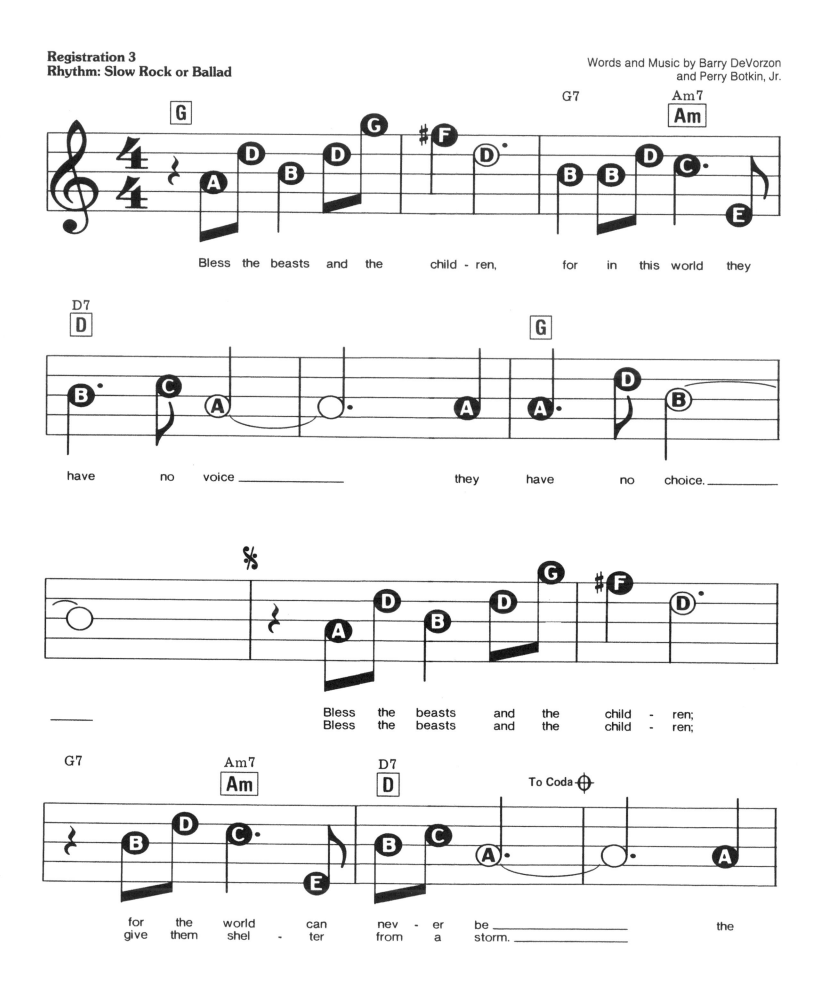

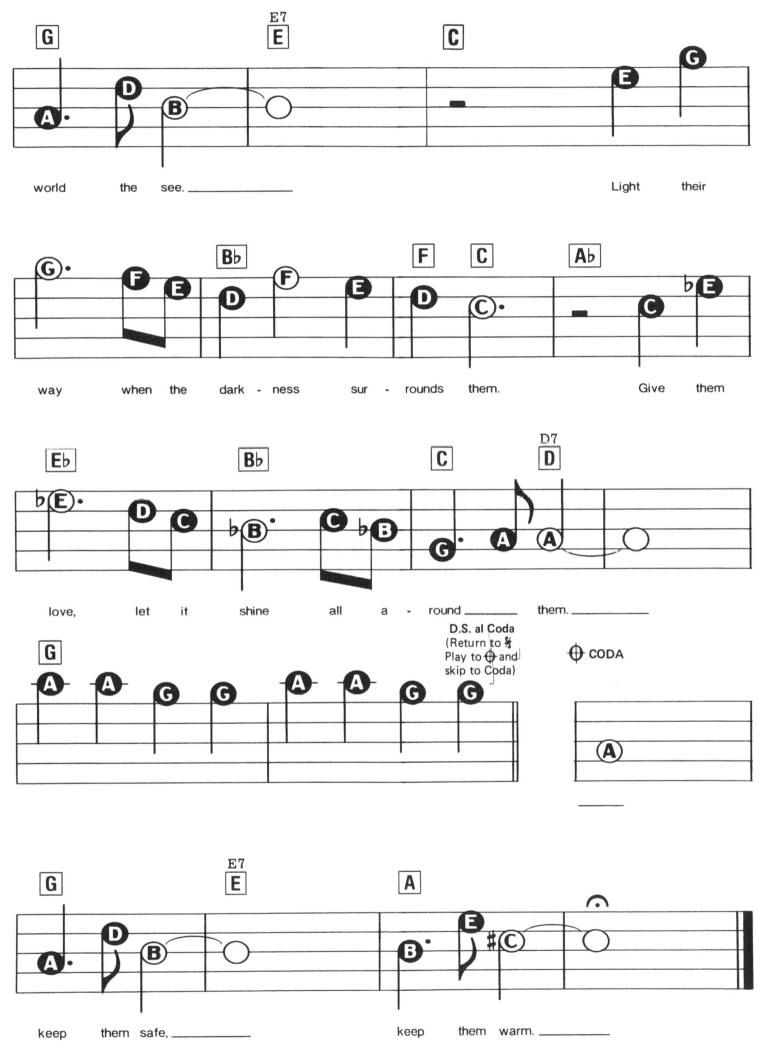

Cherish

Registration 3
Rhythm: Rock or Disco

Words and Music by Terry Kirkman

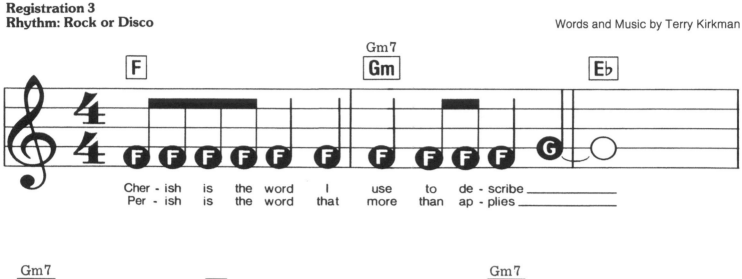

Cher - ish is the word I use to de - scribe _____
Per - ish is the word that more than ap - plies _____

all the feel - ing that I have hid - ing here for you in - side. _____
to the hope _____ in my heart each _____ time I re - a - lize _____

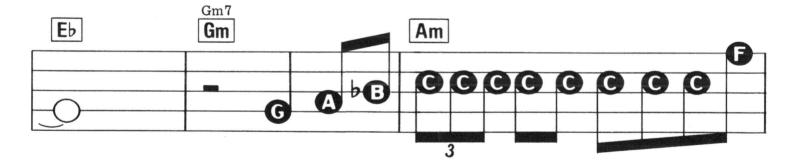

_____ You don't know how man - y times I've wished that I had
_____ That I am not gon - na be the one to share your

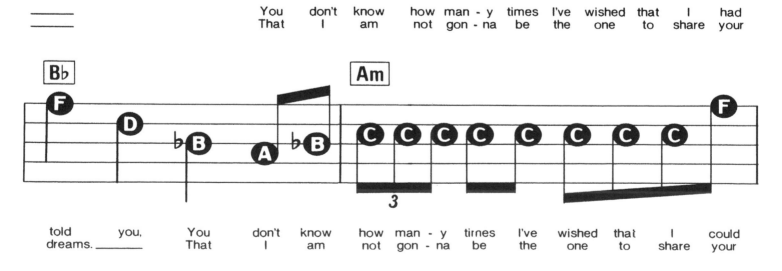

told you, You don't know how man - y times I've wished that I could
dreams. _____ That I am not gon - na be the one to share your

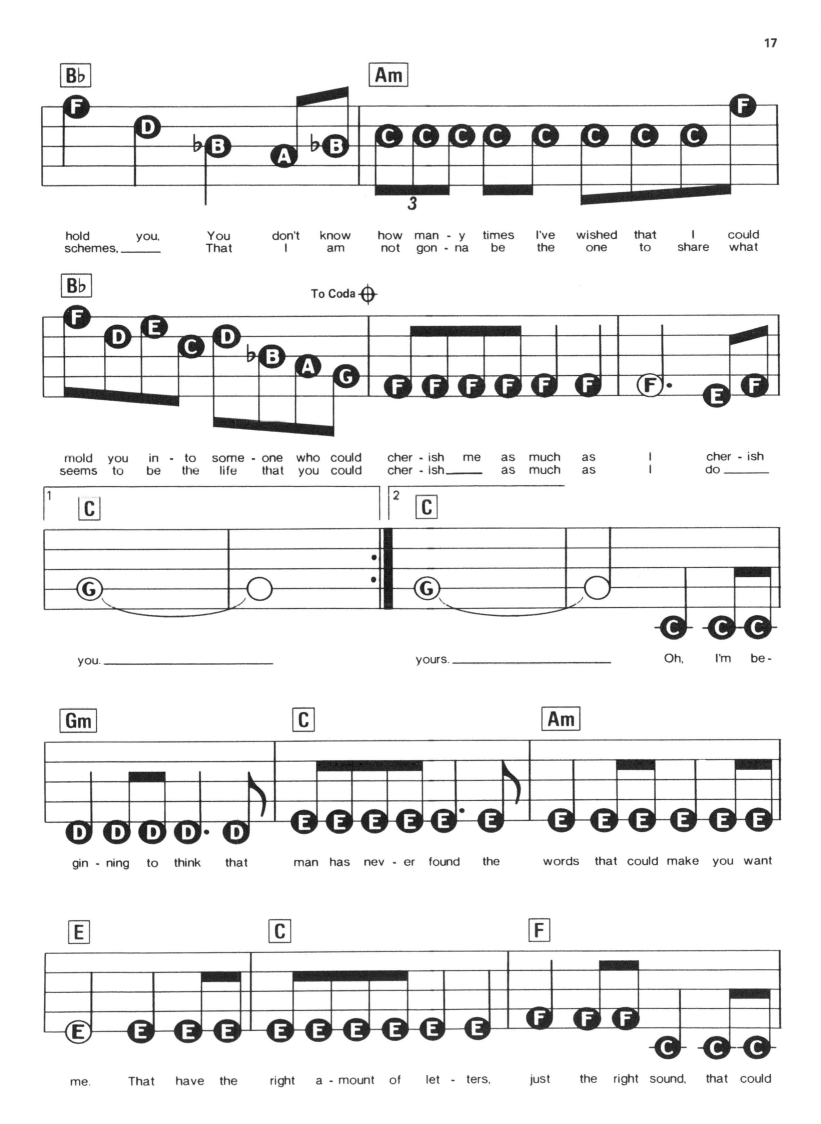

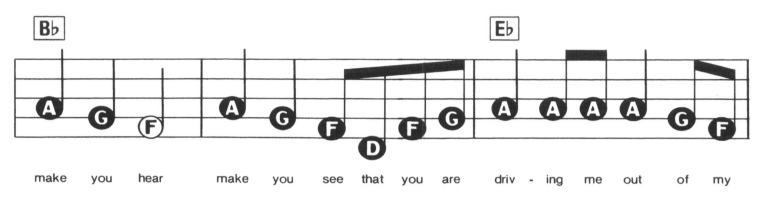

make you hear make you see that you are driv - ing me out of my

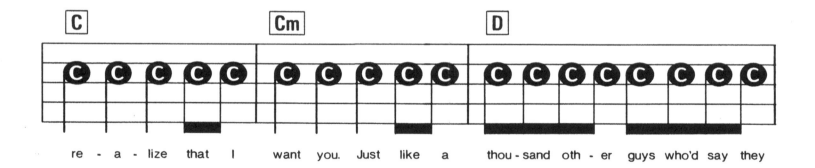

mind._____ Oh, I could say I need you, but then you'd

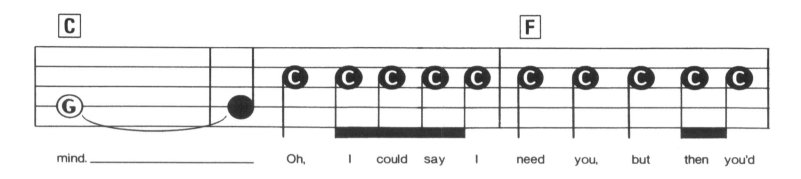

re - a - lize that I want you. Just like a thou - sand oth - er guys who'd say they

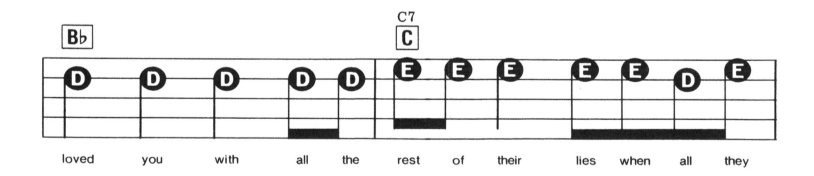

loved you with all the rest of their lies when all they

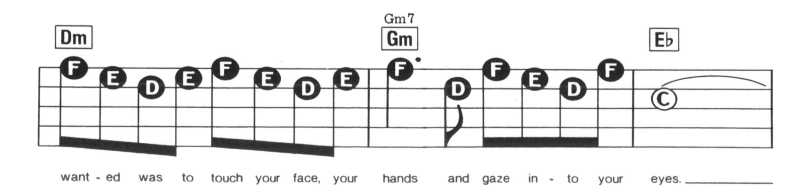

want - ed was to touch your face, your hands and gaze in - to your eyes._____

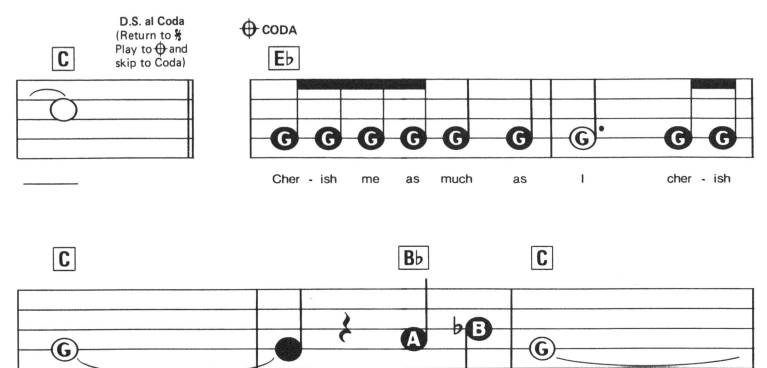

D.S. al Coda
(Return to 𝄋
Play to ⊕ and
skip to Coda)

⊕ CODA

Cher - ish me as much as I cher - ish

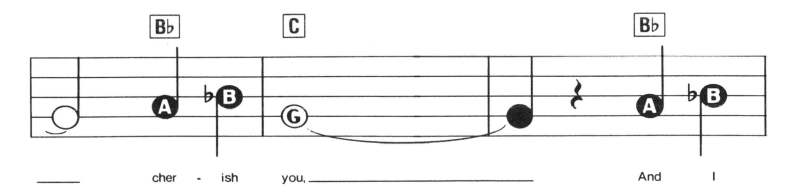

you. _____ And I do _____

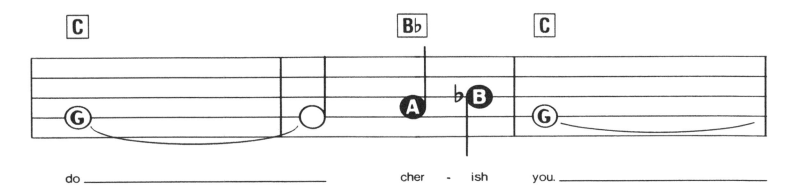

_____ cher - ish you, _____ And I

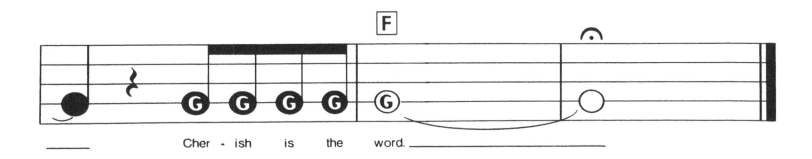

do _____ cher - ish you. _____

Cher - ish is the word. _____

For What It's Worth

Registration 1
Rhythm: Rock or Slow Rock

Words and Music by Stephen Stills

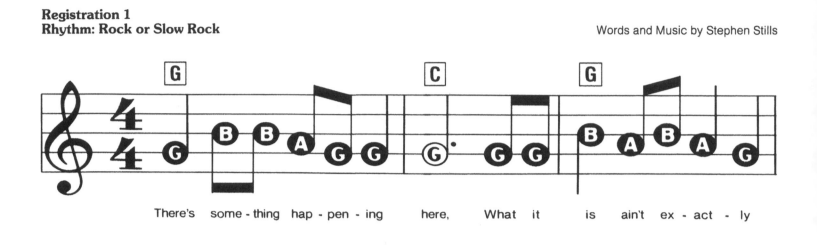

There's some-thing hap-pen-ing here, What it is ain't ex-act-ly

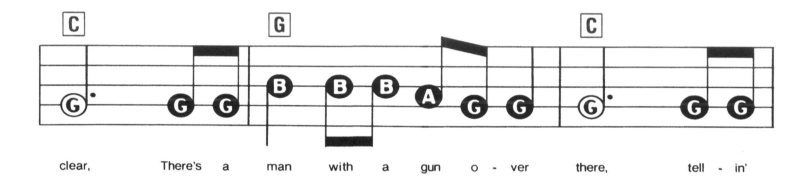

clear, There's a man with a gun o-ver there, tell-in'

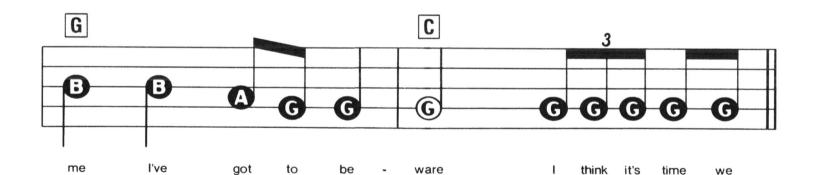

me I've got to be-ware I think it's time we

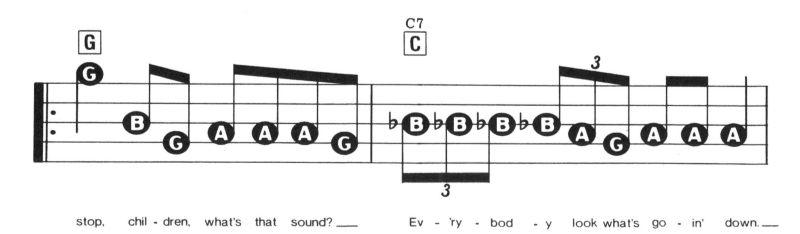

stop, chil-dren, what's that sound? ___ Ev-'ry-bod-y look what's go-in' down. ___

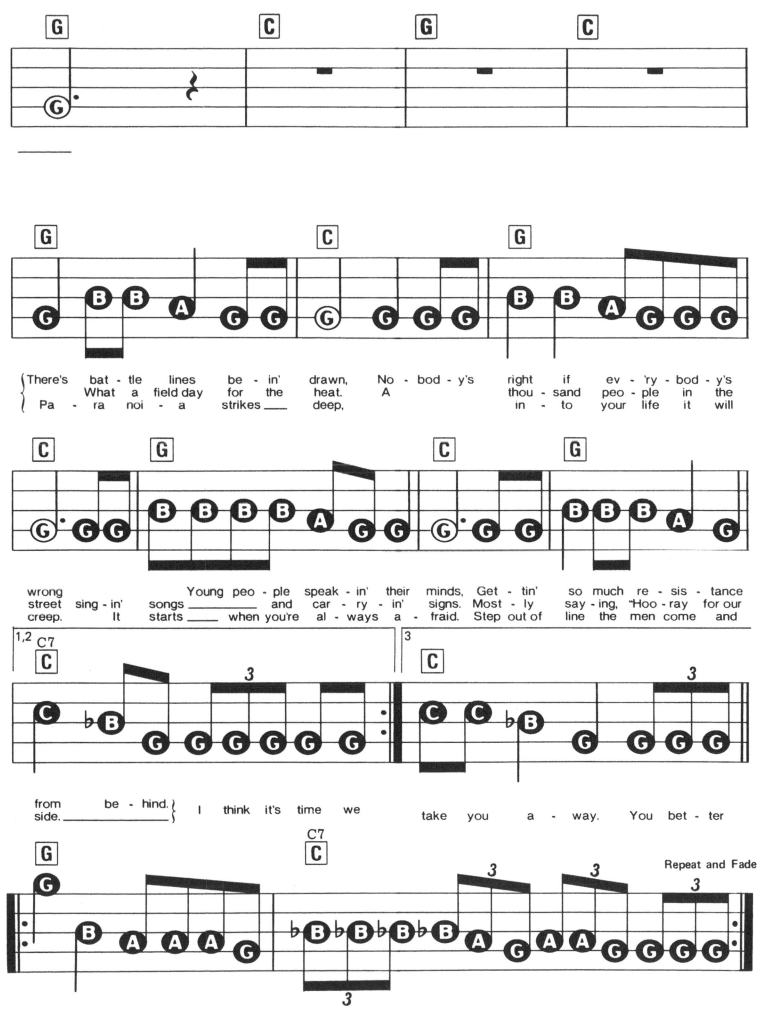

There's bat - tle lines be - in' drawn, No - bod - y's right if ev - 'ry - bod - y's
What a field day for the heat. A thou - sand peo - ple in the
Pa - ra noi - a strikes ____ deep, in - to your life it will

wrong Young peo - ple speak - in' their minds, Get - tin' so much re - sis - tance
street sing - in' songs ____ and car - ry - in' signs. Most - ly say - ing, "Hoo - ray for our
creep. It starts ____ when you're al - ways a - fraid. Step out of line the men come and

from be - hind. I think it's time we take you a - way. You bet - ter
side. ____

stop, hey, what's that sound? ____ Ev - 'ry - bod - y look what's go - in' down. You bet - ter

Haven't Got Time For The Pain

Registration 9
Rhythm: Rock or Disco

Words and Music by Carly Simon
and Jacob Brackman

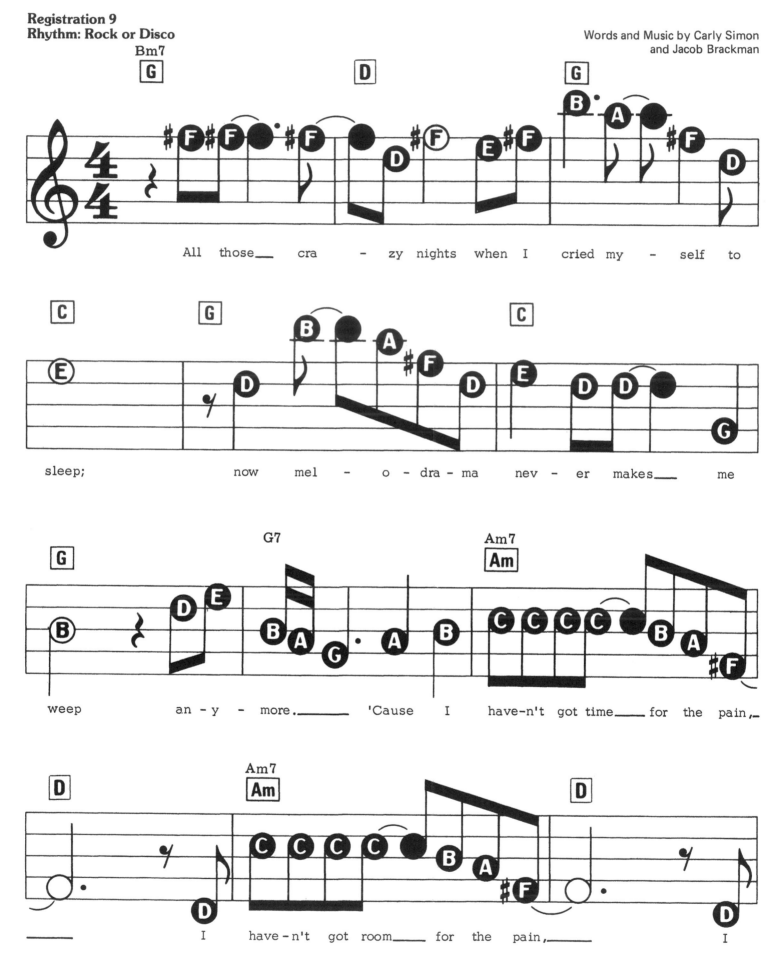

All those__ cra - zy nights when I cried my - self to

sleep; now mel - o - dra - ma nev - er makes__ me

weep an - y - more.__ 'Cause I have-n't got time__ for the pain,__

I have-n't got room__ for the pain,__ I

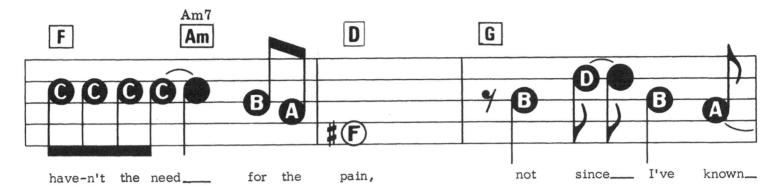

have-n't the need___ for the pain, not since___ I've known___

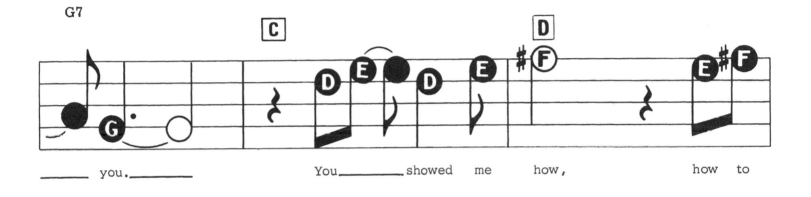

___ you.___ You___ showed me how, how to

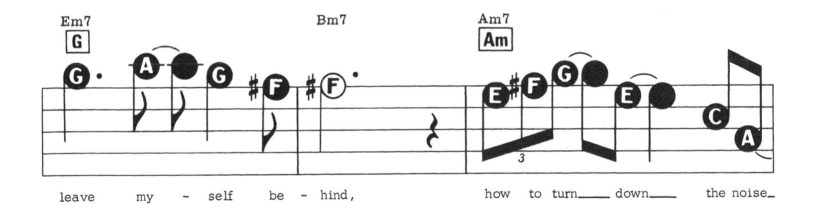

leave my - self be - hind, how to turn___ down___ the noise___

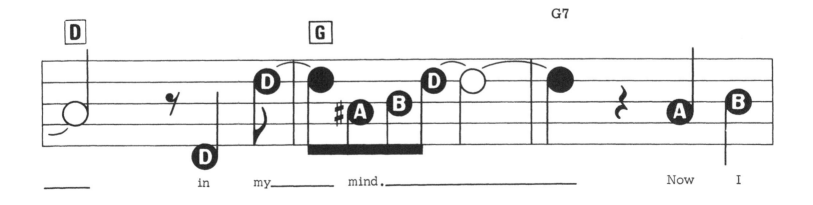

___ in my___ mind.___ Now I

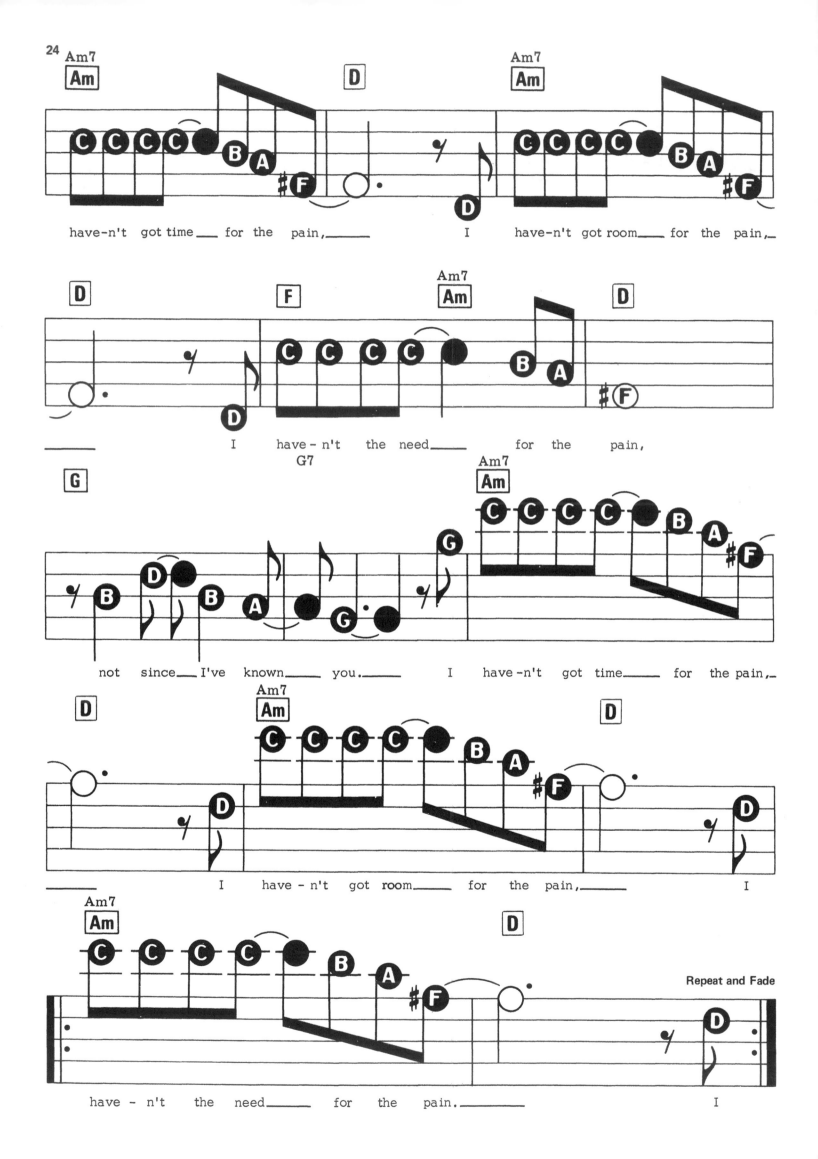

Hotel California

Registration 9
Rhythm: Rock or Disco

Words and Music by Don Henley,
Glenn Frey and Don Felder

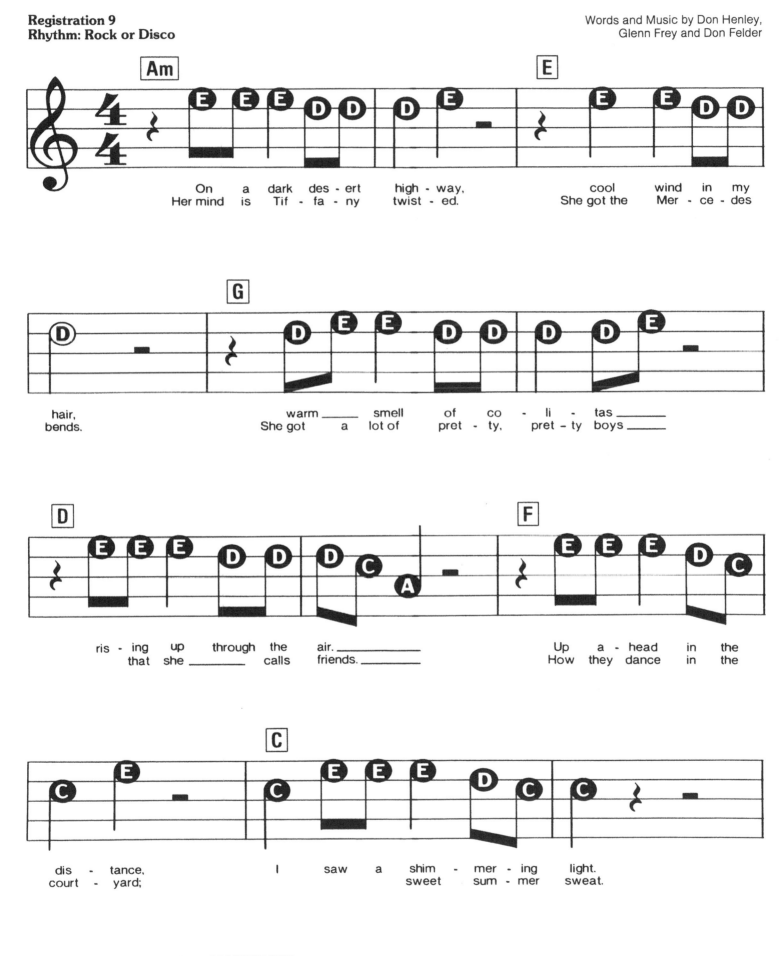

On a dark des - ert high - way, cool wind in my
Her mind is Tif - fa - ny twist - ed. She got the Mer - ce - des

hair, warm _____ smell of co - li - tas _____
bends. She got a lot of pret - ty, pret - ty boys _____

ris - ing up through the air. _____ Up a - head in the
that she _____ calls friends. _____ How they dance in the

dis - tance, I saw a shim - mer - ing light.
court - yard; sweet sum - mer sweat.

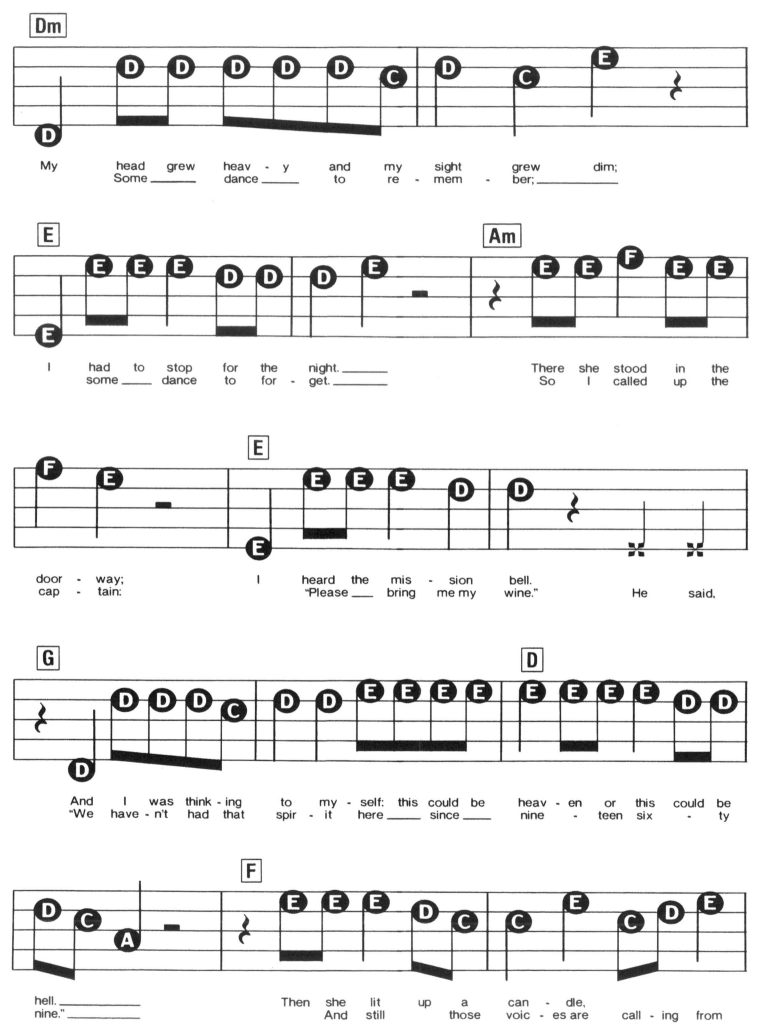

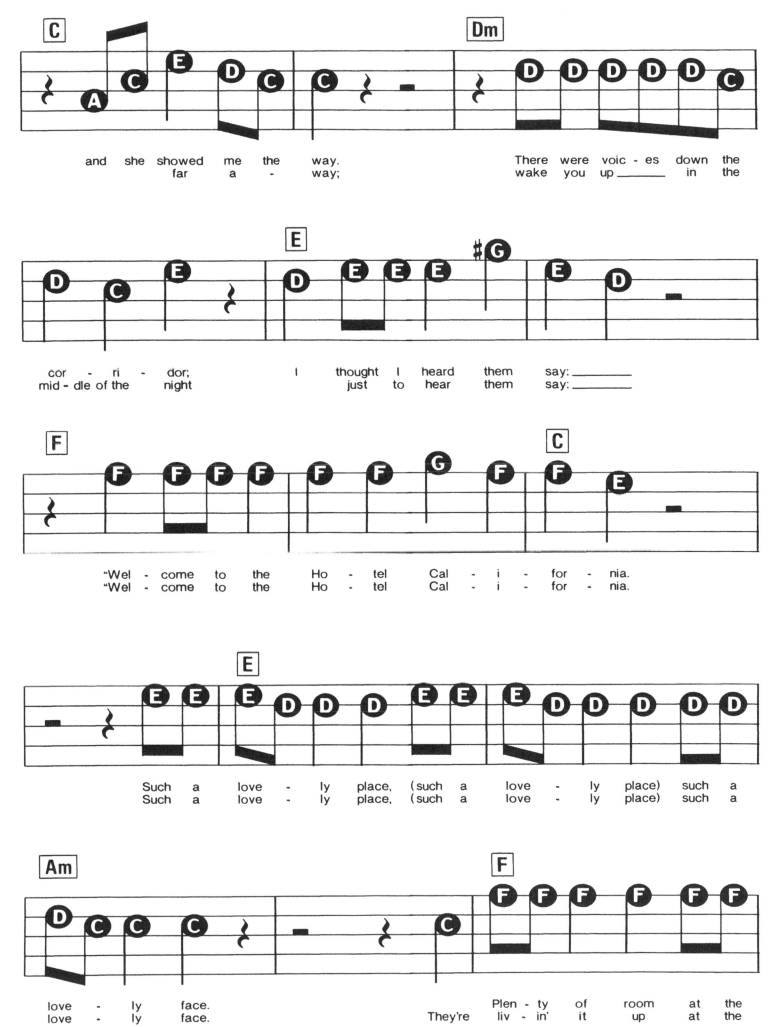

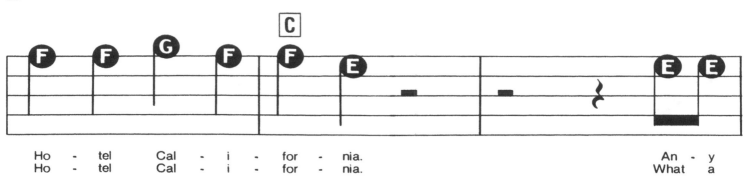

Ho - tel Cal - i - for - nia. An - y
Ho - tel Cal - i - for - nia. What a

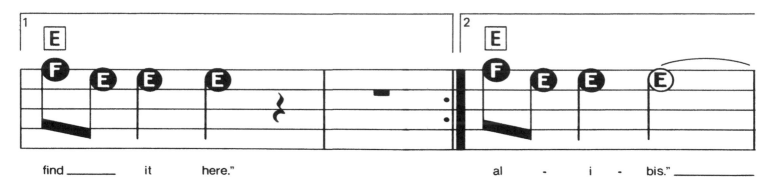

time _____ of year, (an - y time _____ of year) you can
nice _____ sur - prise, (what a nice _____ sur - prise) bring your

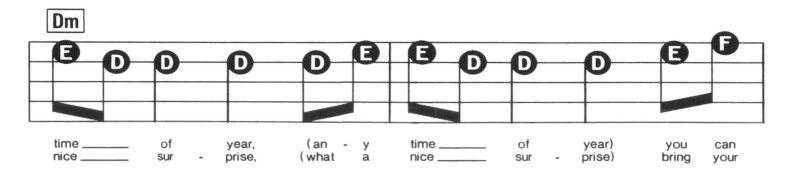

find _____ it here." al - i - bis." _____

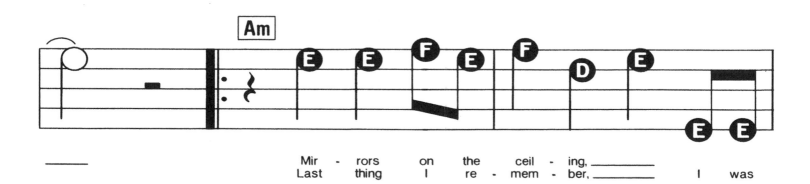

Mir - rors on the ceil - ing, _____ I
Last thing I re - mem - ber, _____ I was

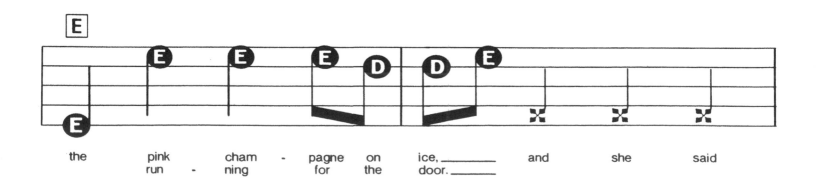

the pink cham - pagne on ice, _____ and she said
run - ning for the door. _____

29

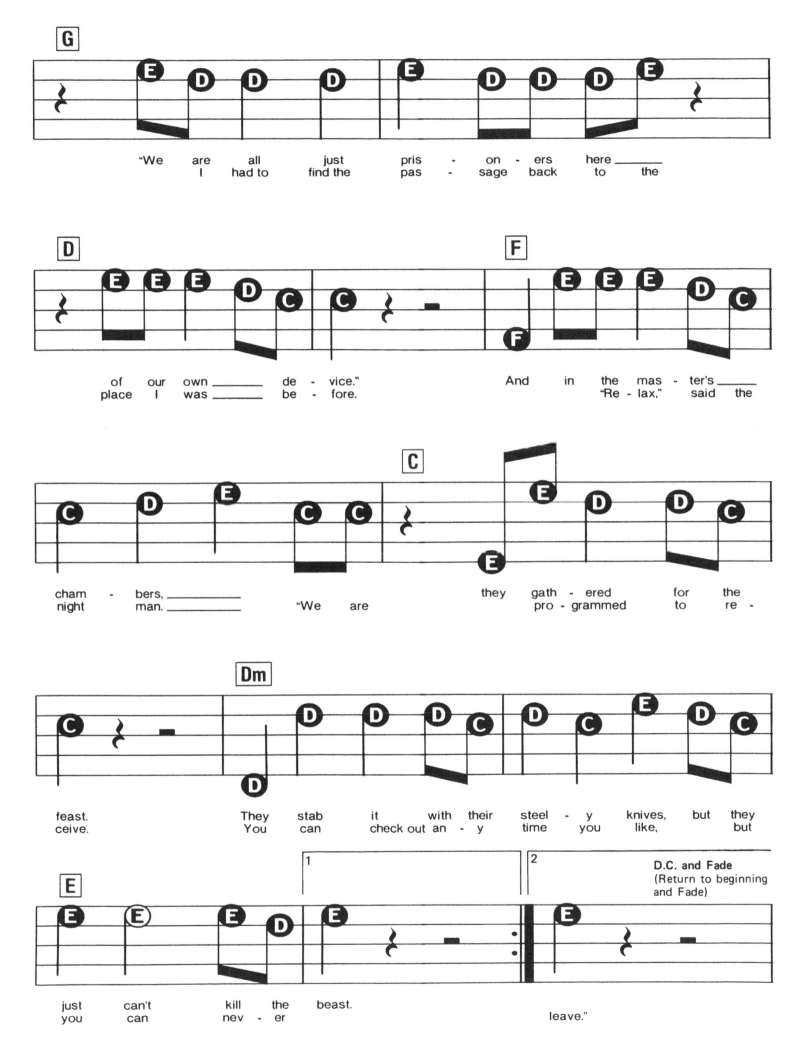

A Horse With No Name

Registration 10
Rhythm: Rock or Slow Rock

Words and Music by
Dewey Bunnell

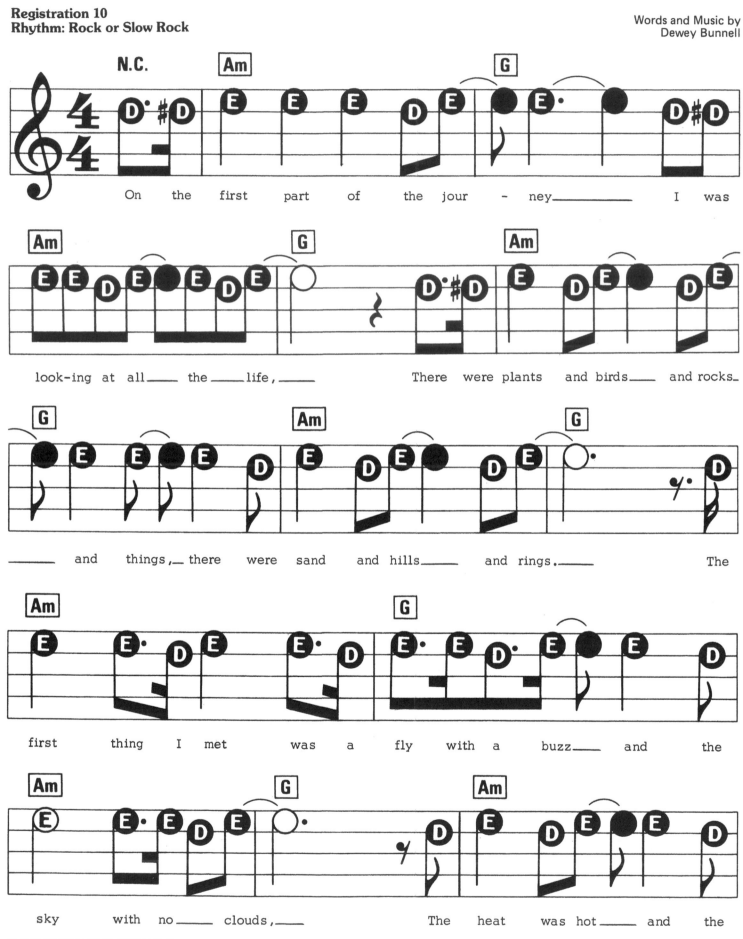

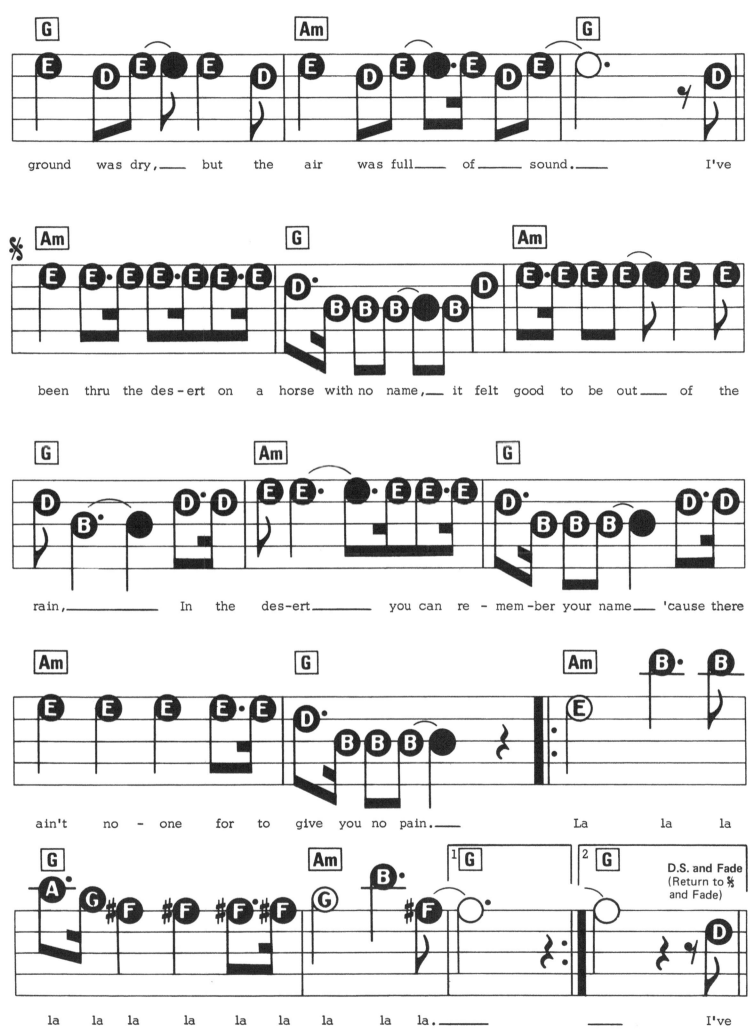

The Hustle

Registration 4
Rhythm: Rock or Disco

Instrumental Music by
Van McCoy

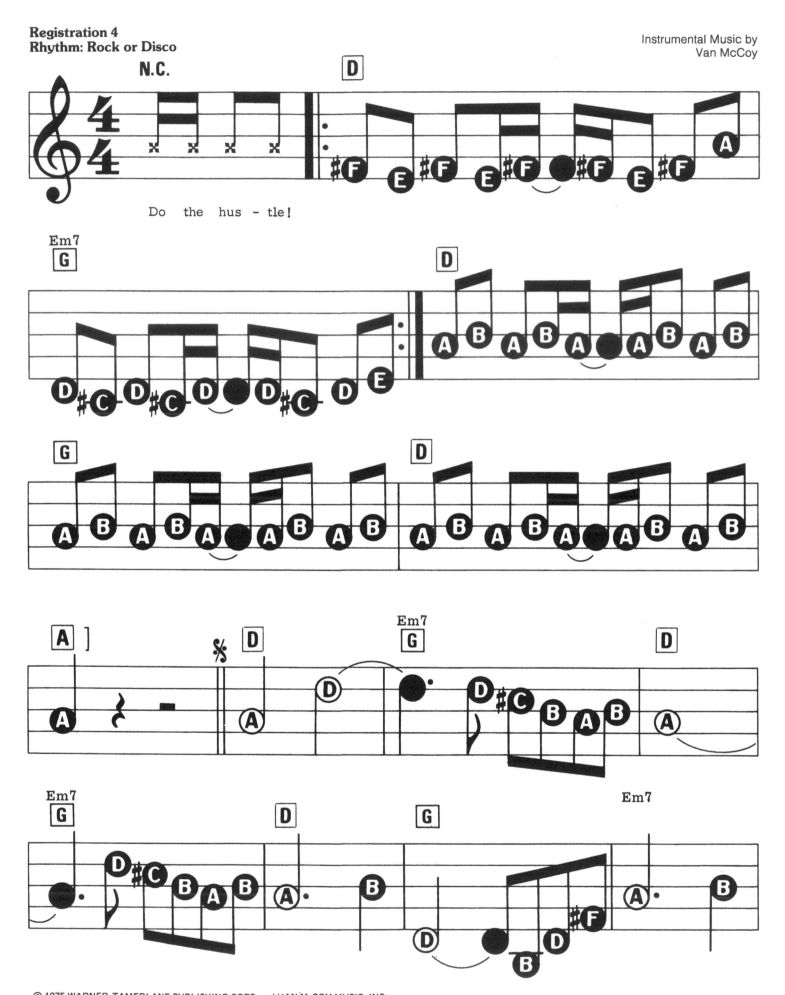

Do the hus - tle!

33

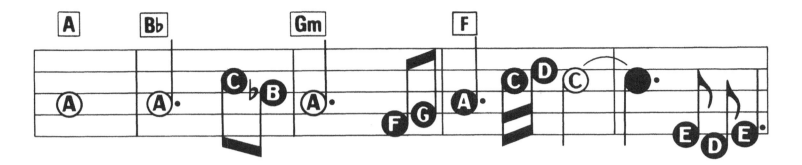

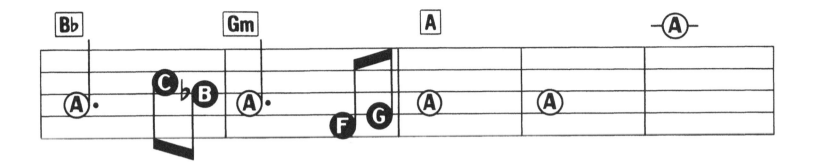

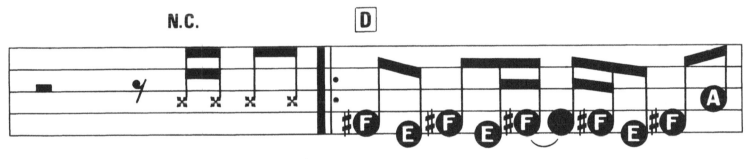

Do the hus - tle!

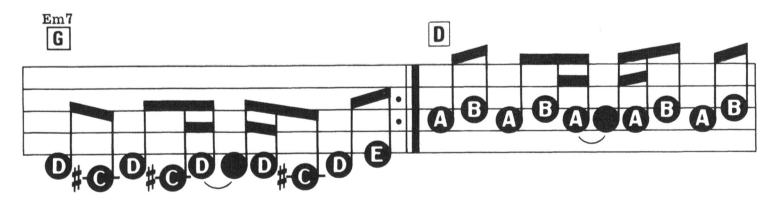

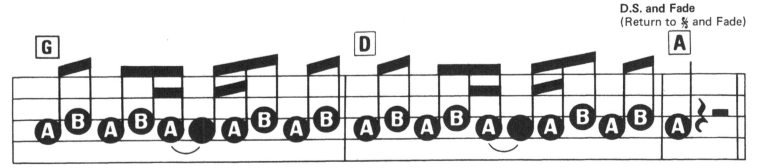

I Believe In Music

Registration 4
Rhythm: Rock or Disco

Words and Music by Mac Davis

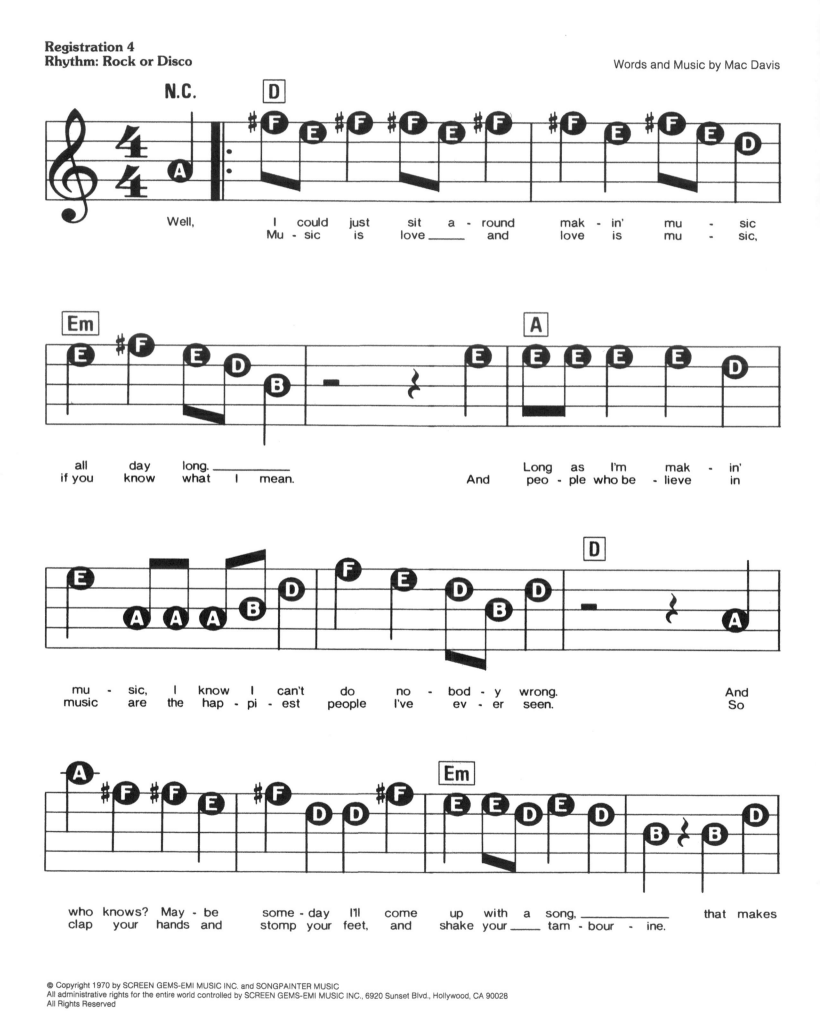

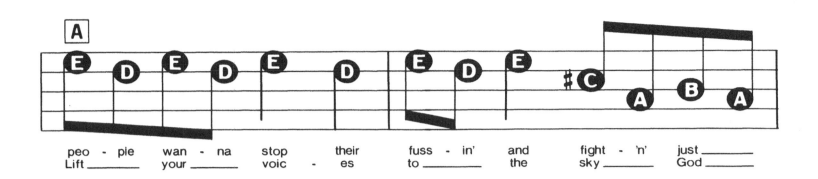

peo - ple wan - na stop their fuss - in' and fight - 'n' just _____
Lift _____ your _____ voic - es to _____ the sky _____ God _____

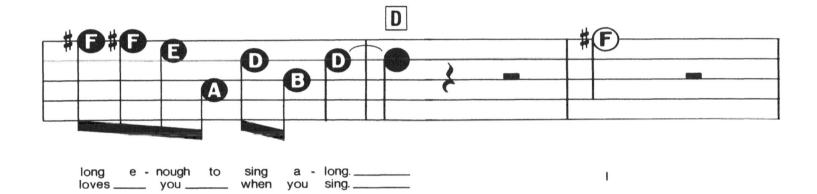

long e - nough to sing a - long._____
loves _____ you _____ when you sing._____

I

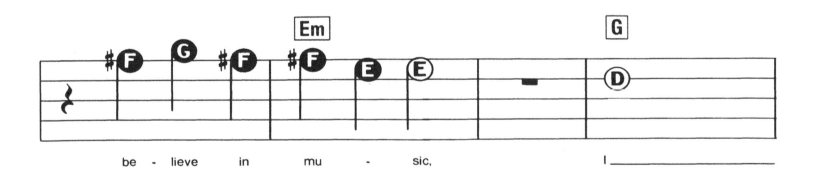

be - lieve in mu - sic, I _____

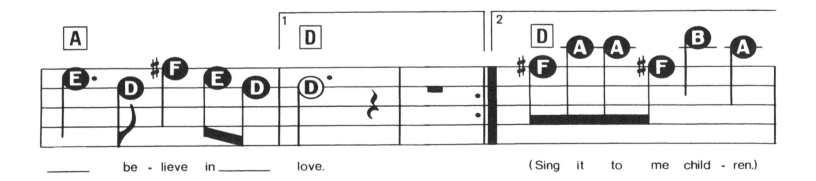

_____ be - lieve in _____ love.

(Sing it to me child - ren.)

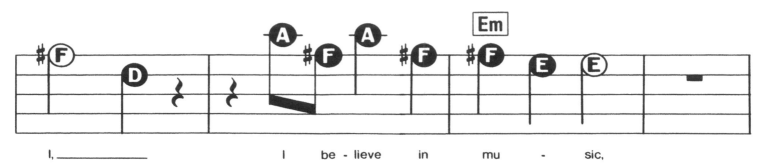

I, _____ I be - lieve in mu - sic,

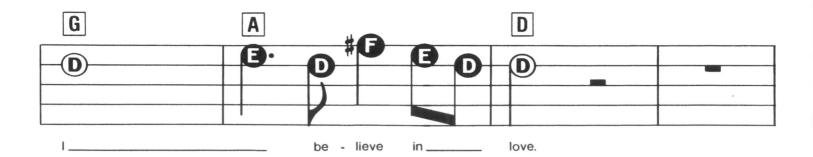

I _____ be - lieve in _____ love.

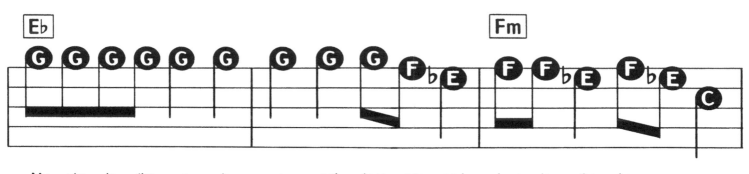

Mu - sic is the un - iv - er - sal lang - uage, and love is the key _____

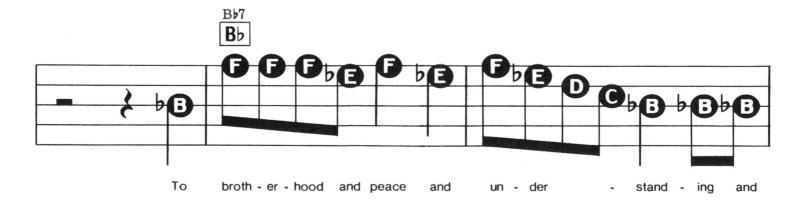

To broth - er - hood and peace and un - der - stand - ing and

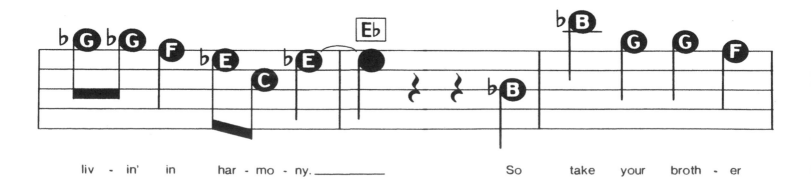

liv - in' in har - mo - ny. _____ So take your broth - er

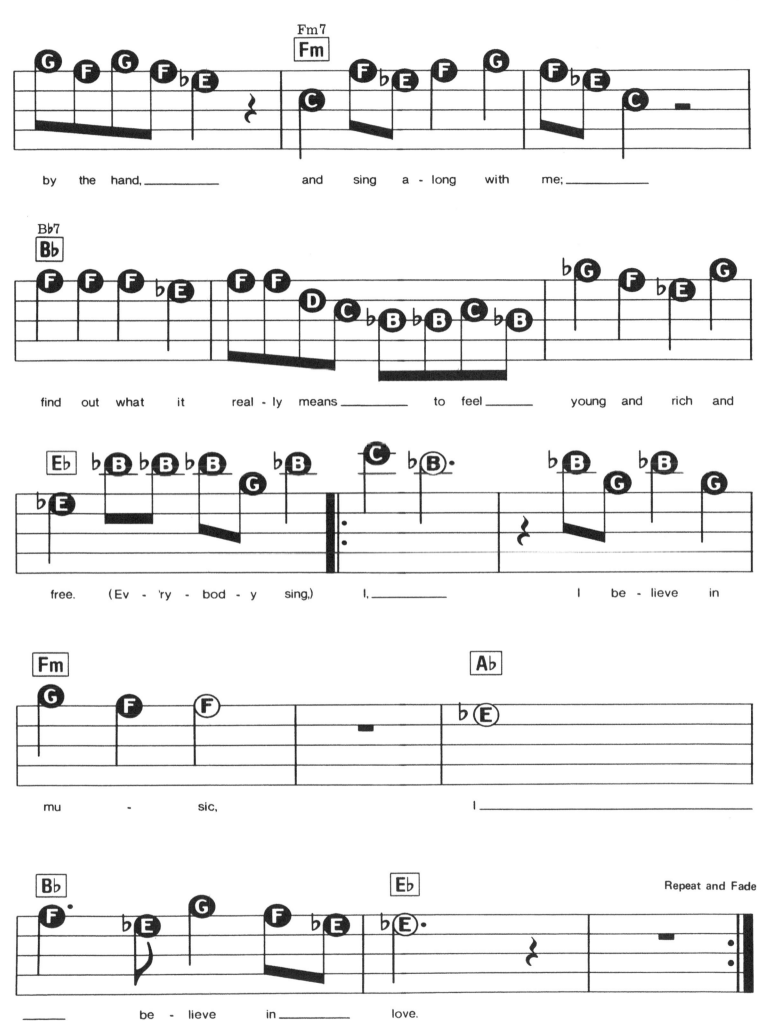

by the hand, _____ and sing a - long with me; _____

find out what it real - ly means _____ to feel _____ young and rich and

free. (Ev - 'ry - bod - y sing,) I, _____ I be - lieve in

mu - sic, I _____

_____ be - lieve in _____ love.

Repeat and Fade

I'll Have To Say I Love You In A Song

Registration 2
Rhythm: Slow Rock or Ballad

Words and Music by
Jim Croce

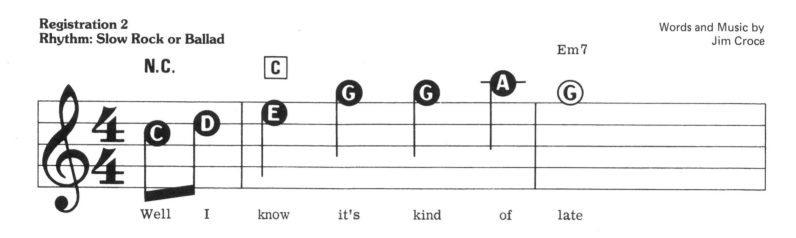

Well I know it's kind of late

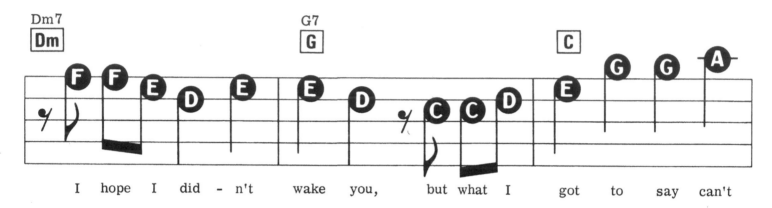

I hope I did-n't wake you, but what I got to say can't

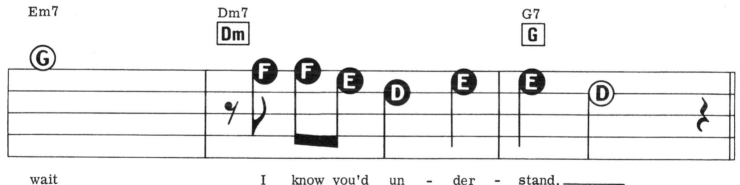

wait   I know you'd un-der-stand._____

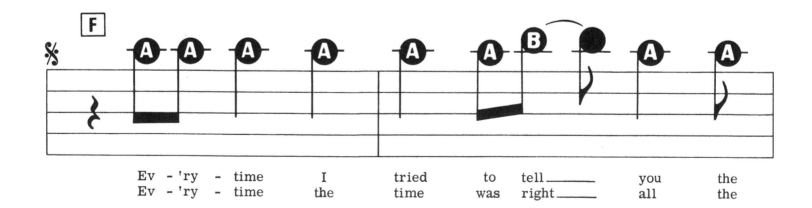

Ev -'ry - time I tried to tell_____ you the
Ev -'ry - time the time was right_____ all the

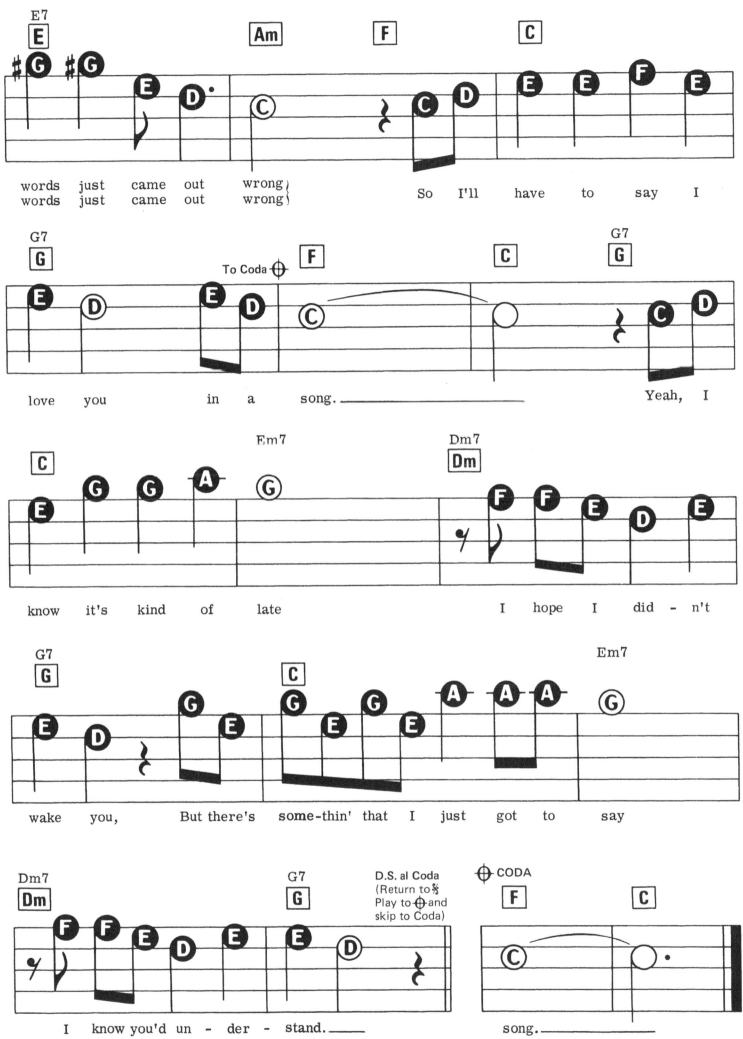

If

Registration 2
Rhythm: Rock or Slow Rock

Words and Music by David Gates

If a pic - ture paints a thou - sand words, then why can't I paint
man could be two plac - es at one time I'd be with

you? The words will nev - er show the you I've come to know.
you To - mor - row and to - day, be - side you all the way.

If a face could launch a thou - sand ships, then where am I to
If the world should stop re - volv - ing, spin - ning slow - ly down to

go? There's no one home but you; you're all that's left me,
die, I'd spend the end with you you and when the world was

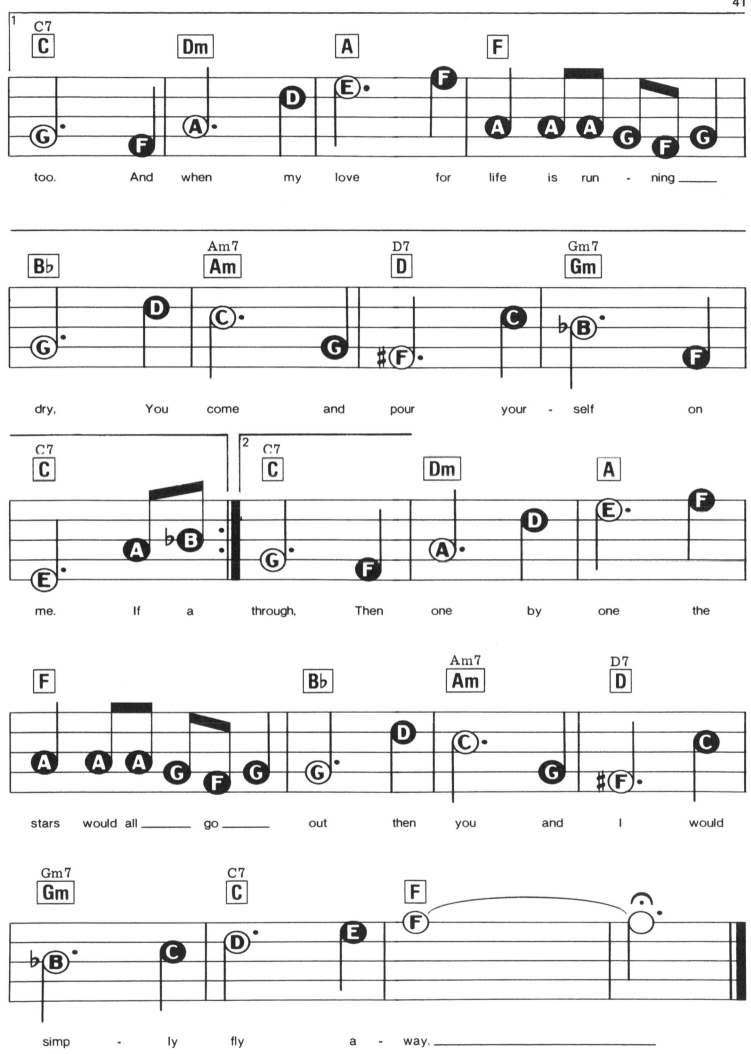

If You Could Read My Mind

Registration 5
Rhythm: Rock or Slow Rock

Words and Music by Gordon Lightfoot

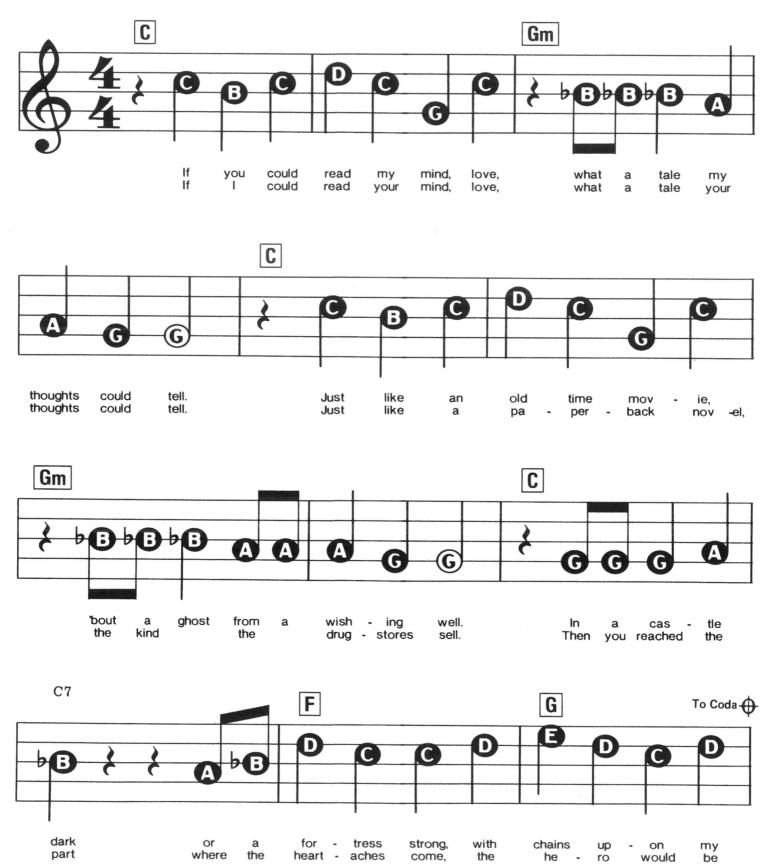

If you could read my mind, love, what a tale my
If I could read your mind, love, what a tale your

thoughts could tell. Just like an old time mov - ie,
thoughts could tell. Just like a pa - per - back nov - el,

'bout a ghost from a wish - ing well. In a cas - tle
the kind from the drug - stores sell. Then you reached the

dark or a for - tress strong, with chains up - on my
part where the heart - aches come, with the he - ro would be

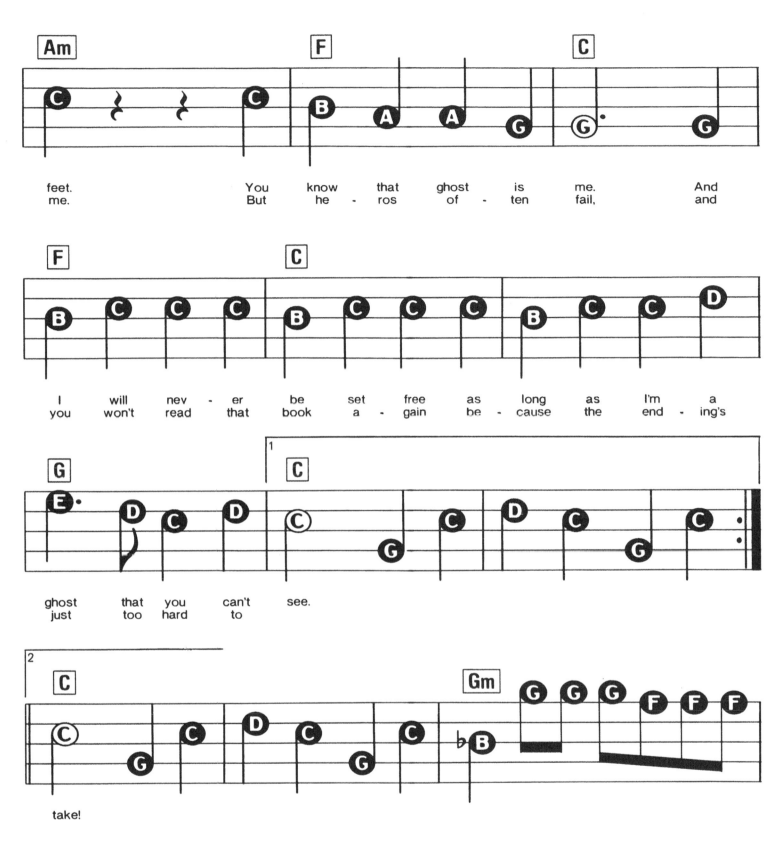

feet.
me.

You
But

know
he -

that
ros

ghost
of -

is
ten

me.
fail,

And
and

I
you

will
won't

nev -
read

er
that

be
book

set
a -

free
gain

as
be -

long
cause

as
the

I'm
end -

a
ing's

ghost
just

that
too

you
hard

can't
to

see.

take!

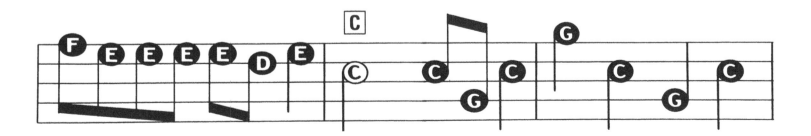

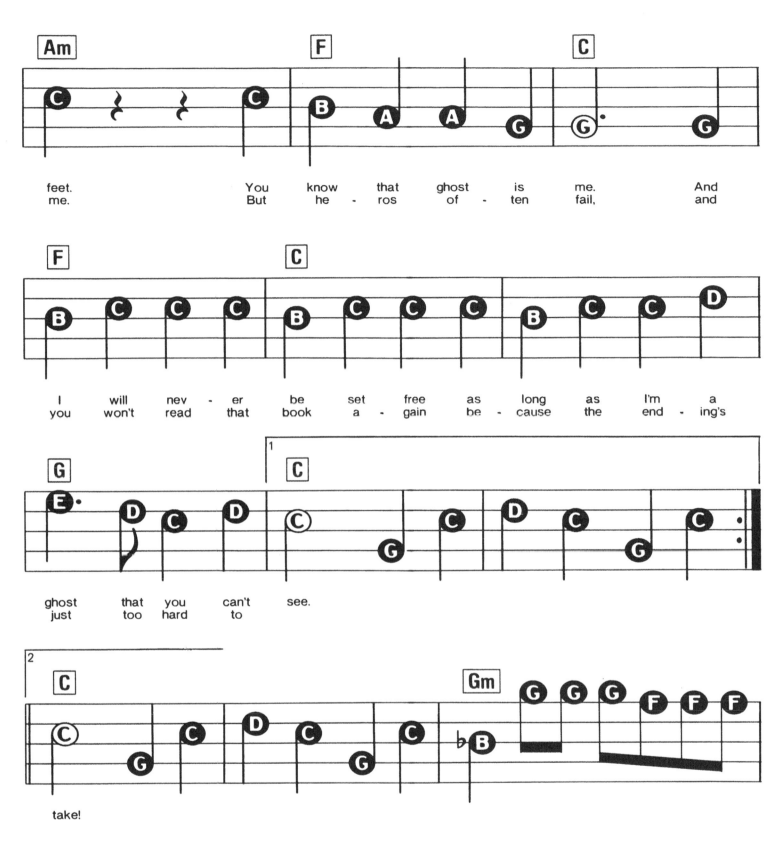

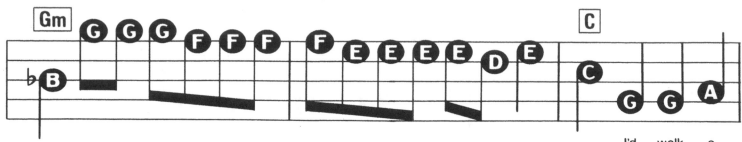

I'd walk a-

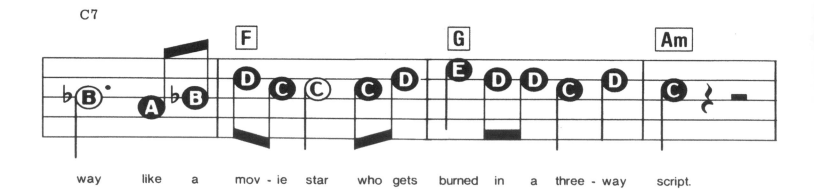

way like a mov - ie star who gets burned in a three - way script.

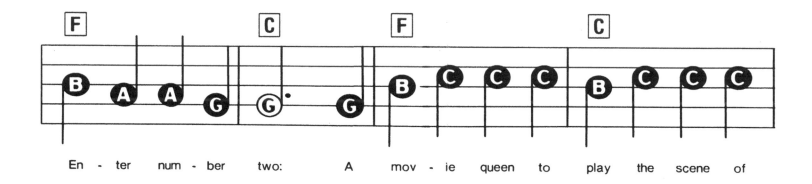

En - ter num - ber two: A mov - ie queen to play the scene of

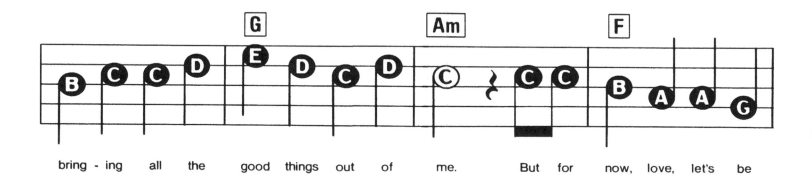

bring - ing all the good things out of me. But for now, love, let's be

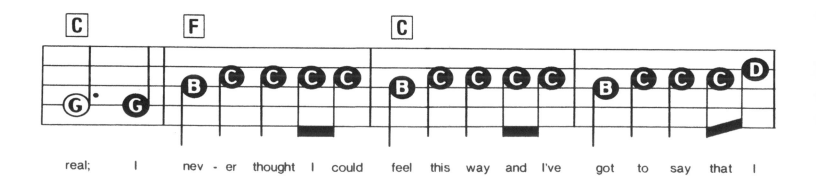

real; I nev - er thought I could feel this way and I've got to say that I

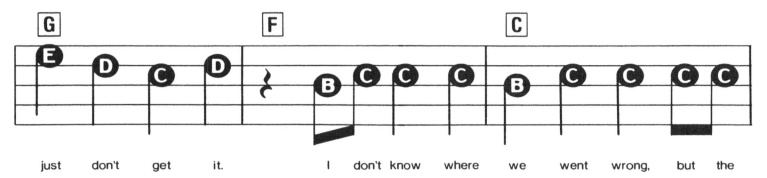

just don't get it.　　　I don't know where we went wrong, but the

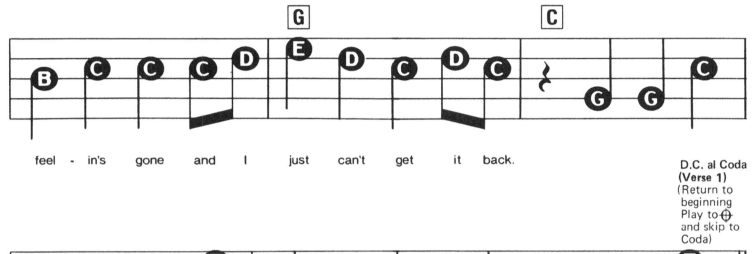

feel - in's gone and I just can't get it back.

D.C. al Coda
(Verse 1)
(Return to beginning Play to ⊕ and skip to Coda)

⊕ CODA

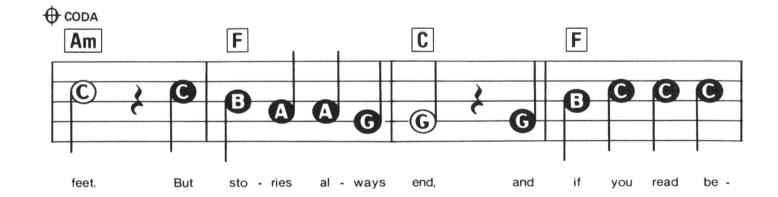

feet.　　But sto - ries al - ways end,　　and if you read be -

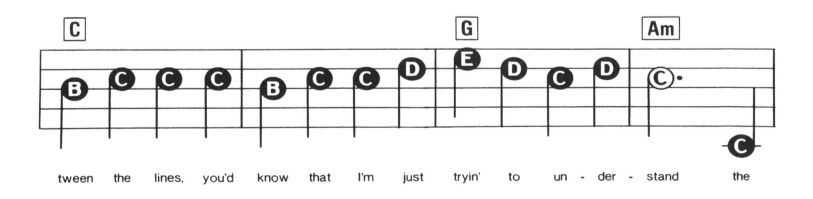

tween the lines, you'd know that I'm just tryin' to un - der - stand the

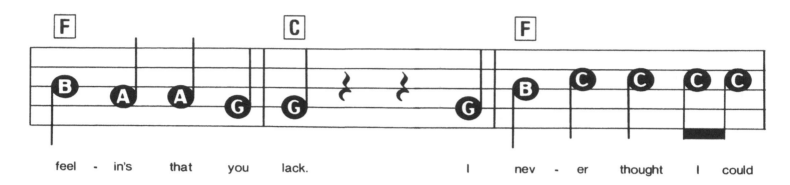

feel - in's that you lack. I nev - er thought I could

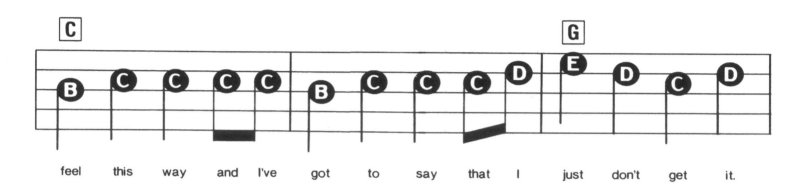

feel this way and I've got to say that I just don't get it.

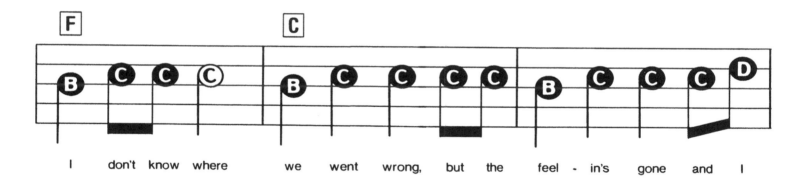

I don't know where we went wrong, but the feel - in's gone and I

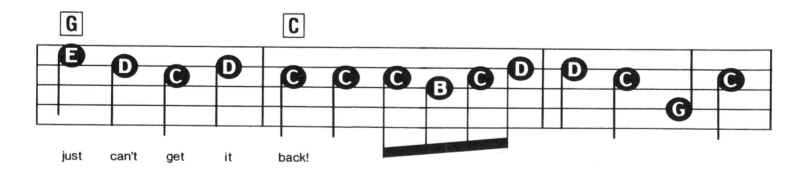

just can't get it back!

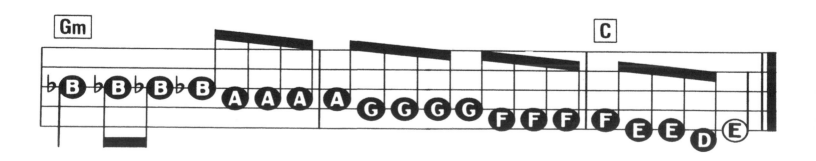

The Main Event

(First Artists Presents A Jon Peters Production of a Barwood Film - "THE MAIN EVENT")

Registration 9
Rhythm: Rock or Disco

Words and Music by
Paul Jabara and Bruce Roberts

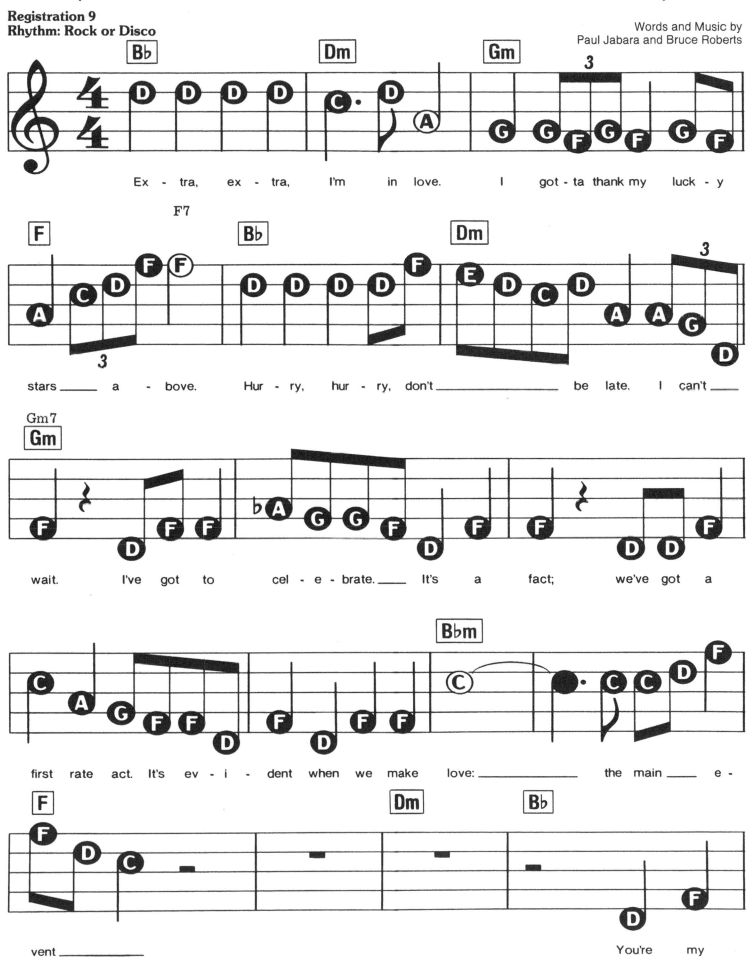

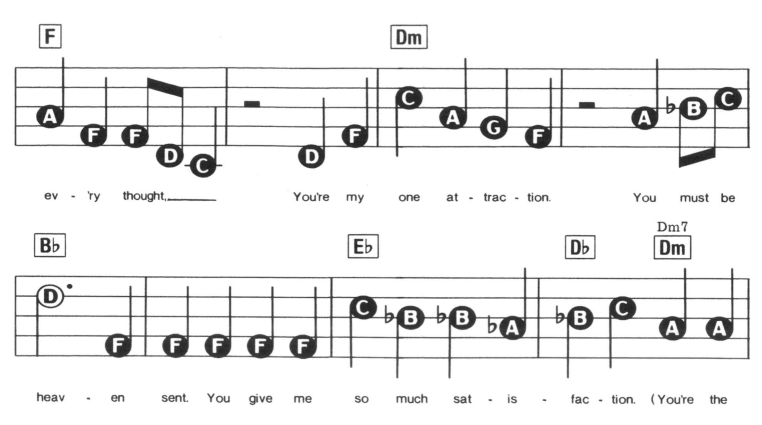

ev - 'ry thought,_____ You're my one at - trac - tion. You must be

heav - en sent. You give me so much sat - is - fac - tion. (You're the

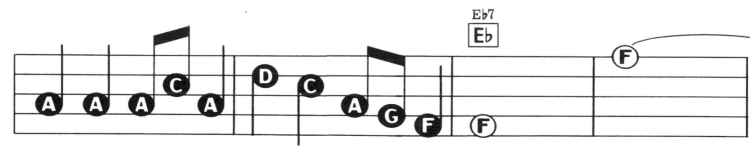

one.) You make life worth fight - ing for. You're the one._____

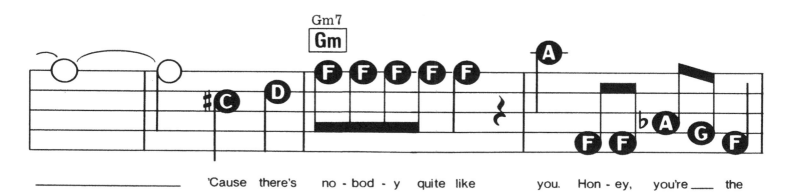

_____ 'Cause there's no - bod - y quite like you. Hon - ey, you're____ the

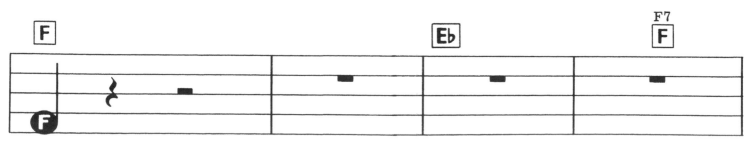

one.

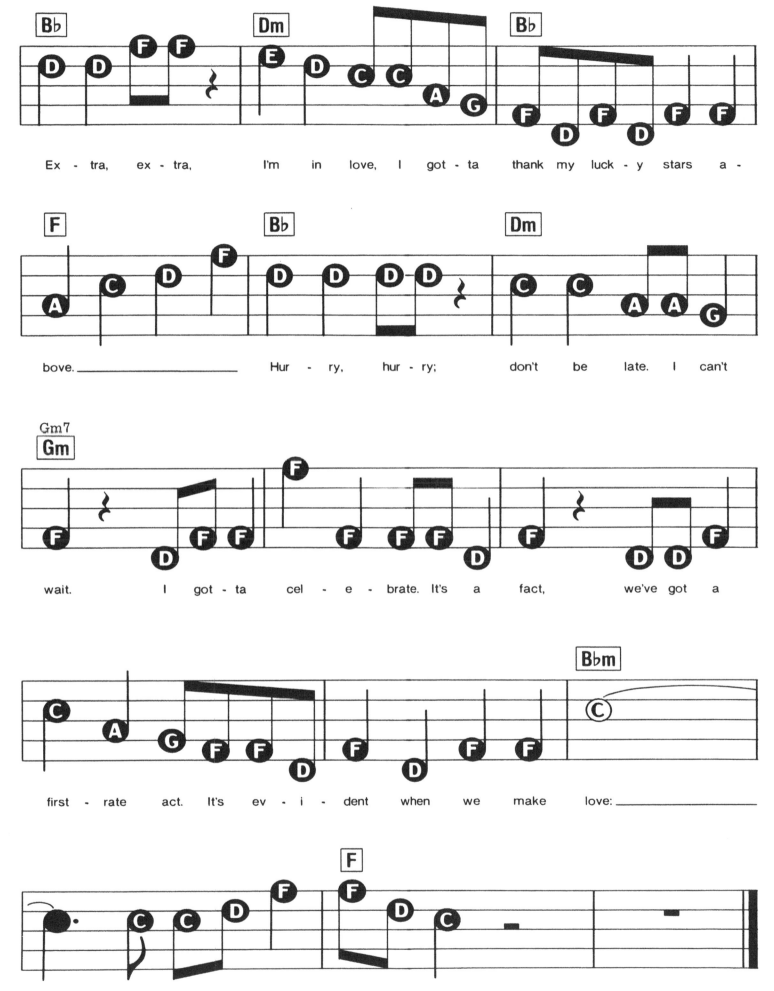

Lyin' Eyes

Registration 2
Rhythm: Rock or Slow Rock

Words and Music by Don Henley
and Glenn Frey

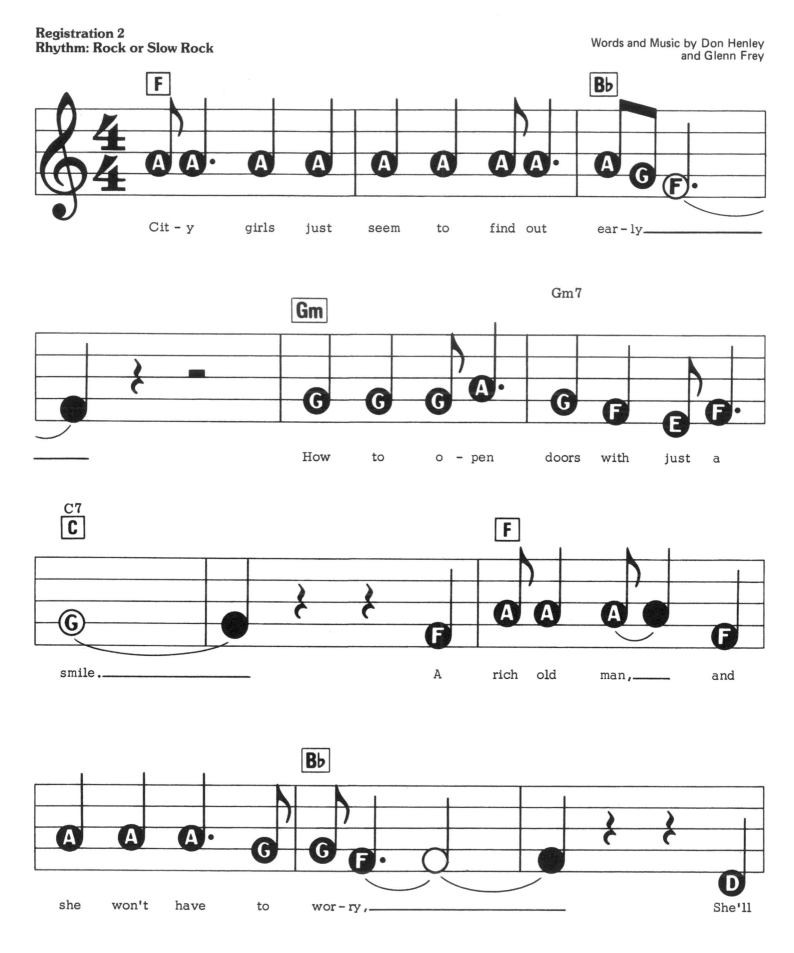

Cit - y girls just seem to find out ear - ly_____

_____ How to o - pen doors with just a

smile._____ A rich old man,_____ and

she won't have to wor - ry,_____ She'll

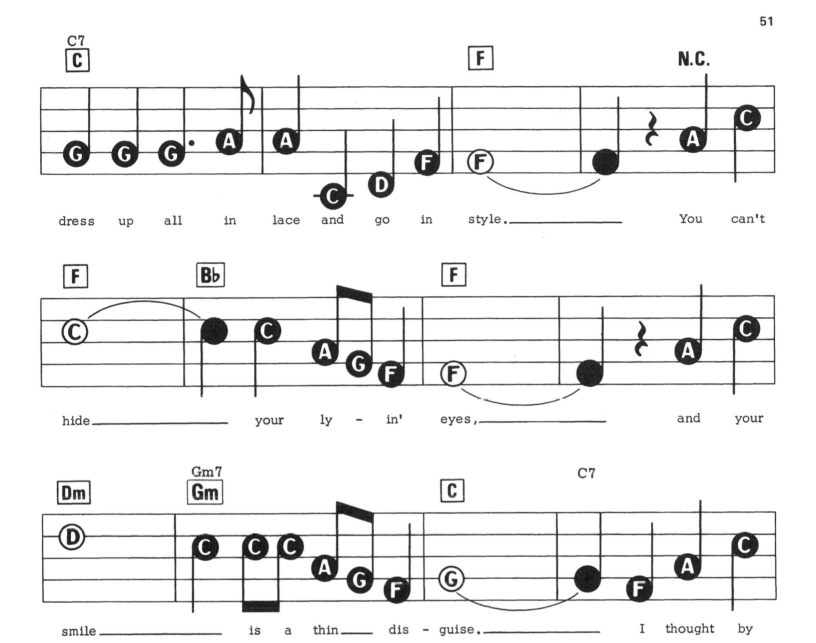

dress up all in lace and go in style.＿＿＿＿ You can't

hide＿＿＿＿ your ly - in' eyes,＿＿＿＿ and your

smile＿＿＿＿ is a thin＿ dis - guise.＿＿＿＿ I thought by

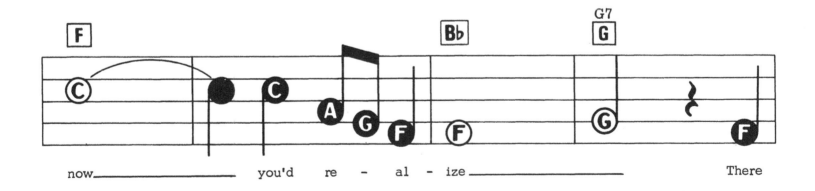

now＿＿＿＿ you'd re - al - ize＿＿＿＿ There

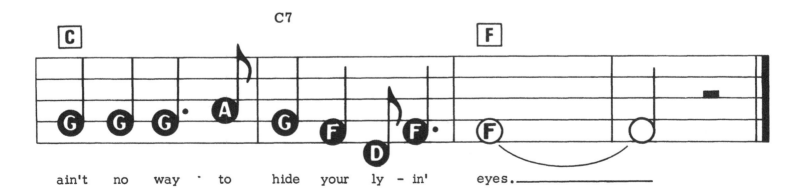

ain't no way to hide your ly - in' eyes.＿＿＿＿

Mr. Bojangles

Registration 3
Rhythm: Waltz

Words and Music by
Jerry Jeff Walker

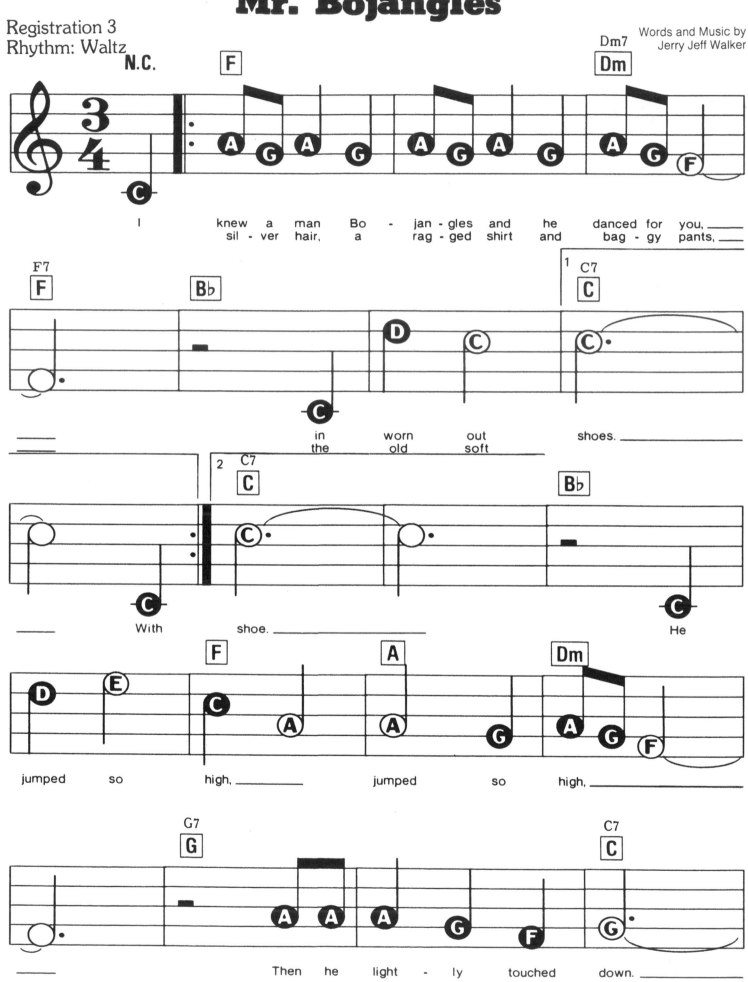

I knew a man Bo - jan - gles and he danced for you, _____
sil - ver hair, a rag - ged shirt and bag - gy pants, _____

_____ in the worn out old soft shoes. _____

With shoe. _____ He

jumped so high, _____ jumped so high, _____

Then he light - ly touched down. _____

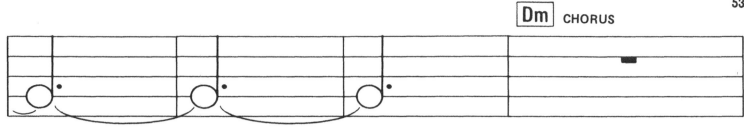

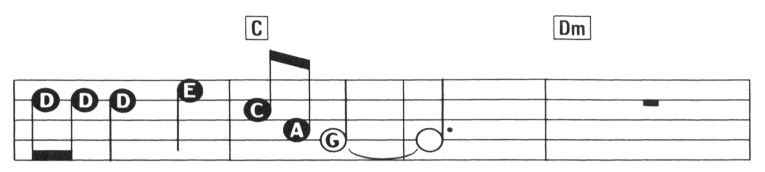

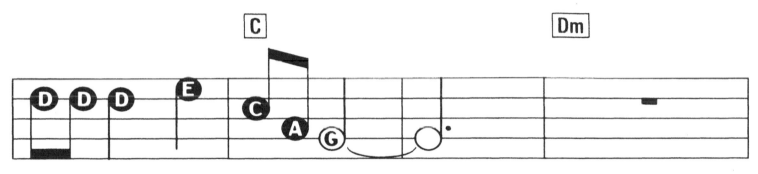

Mis - ter Bo - jan - gles, _____

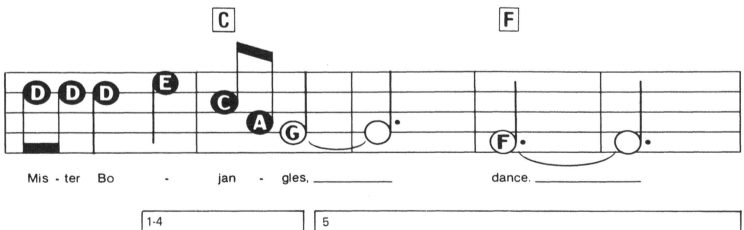

Mis - ter Bo - jan - gles, _____

Mis - ter Bo - jan - gles, _____ dance. _____

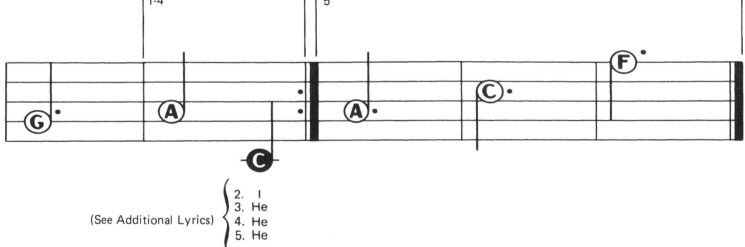

(See Additional Lyrics)
2. I
3. He
4. He
5. He

Additional Lyrics

Verse 2   I met him in a cell in New Orleans
I was down and out.
He looked at me to be the eyes of age
As he spoke right out.
He talked of life, talked of life,
He laughed slapped his leg a step.
(Chorus)

Verse 3   He said his name, Bojangles,
Then he danced a lick across the cell.
He grabbed his pants a better stance
Oh, he jumped up high,
He clicked his heels.
He let go a laugh, let go a laugh,
Shook back his clothes all around
(Chorus)

Verse 4   He danced for those at minstrel shows
And county fairs throughout the South.
He spoke with tears of fifteen years
How his dog and he traveled about.
His dog up and died, he up and died,
After twenty years he still grieved.
(Chorus)

Verse 5   He said, "I dance now at every chance
In honky tonks for drinks and tips.
But most of the time I spend behind these county bars."
He said, "I drinks a bit."
He shook his head
And as he shook his head, I heard someone ask please
(Chorus)

Rhiannon

Registration 9
Rhythm: Disco

Words and Music by Stevie Nicks

N.C. Dm

D F G A G G F E D D C

Rhi - an - non rings like a bell through the night. And
She is like a cat in the dark, And and

Bb

D D E F E E D

Dm

F G A A G F

would - n't you love to love her?
then she is to the dark - ness.

Takes to the sky like a
She rules her life like a

Bb

F E D C D E F E E D

bird in flight. And who will be her lov - er?
fine sky - lark And and when the sky is star - less.

F

C D F D C bA G F F bA

Bb

G F C F F D

All your life, you've nev - er seen _____ a wom - an _____ tak - en by the

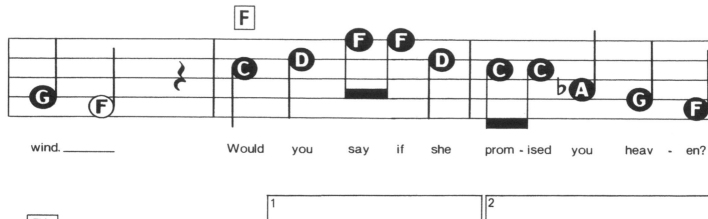

wind. _____ Would you say if she prom - ised you heav - en?

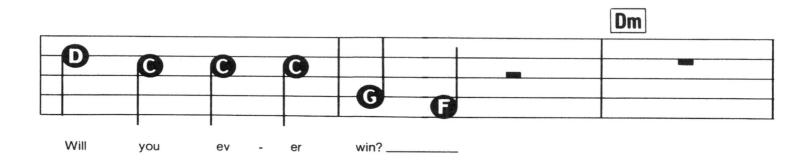

Will you ev - er win? _____ win? _____

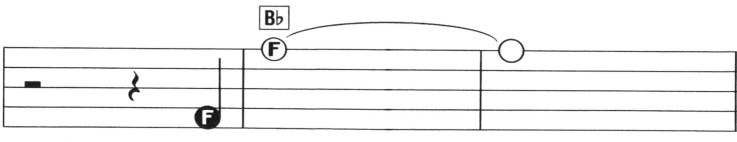

Will you ev - er win? _____

Rhi - an -

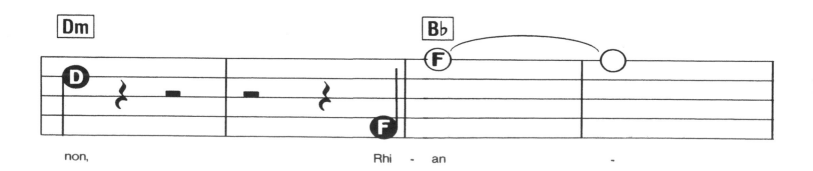

non, Rhi - an -

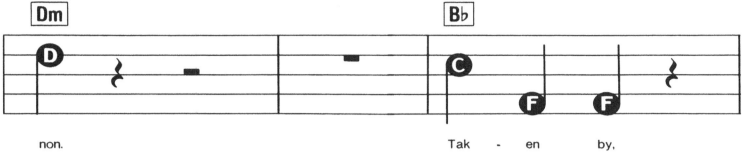

non. Tak - en by,

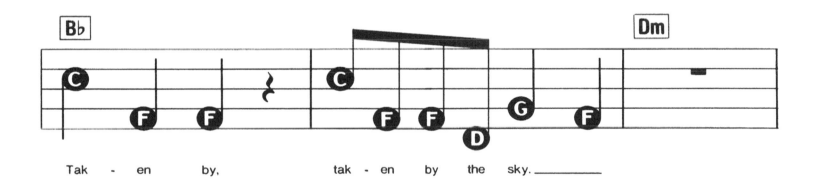

tak - en by the sky. _____

Tak - en by, tak - en by the sky. _____

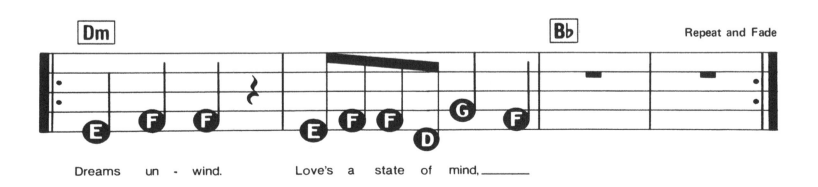

Dreams un - wind. Love's a state of mind, _____

Repeat and Fade

Never My Love

Registration 10
Rhythm: Slow Rock or Rhumba

Words and Music by Don and Dick Addrisi

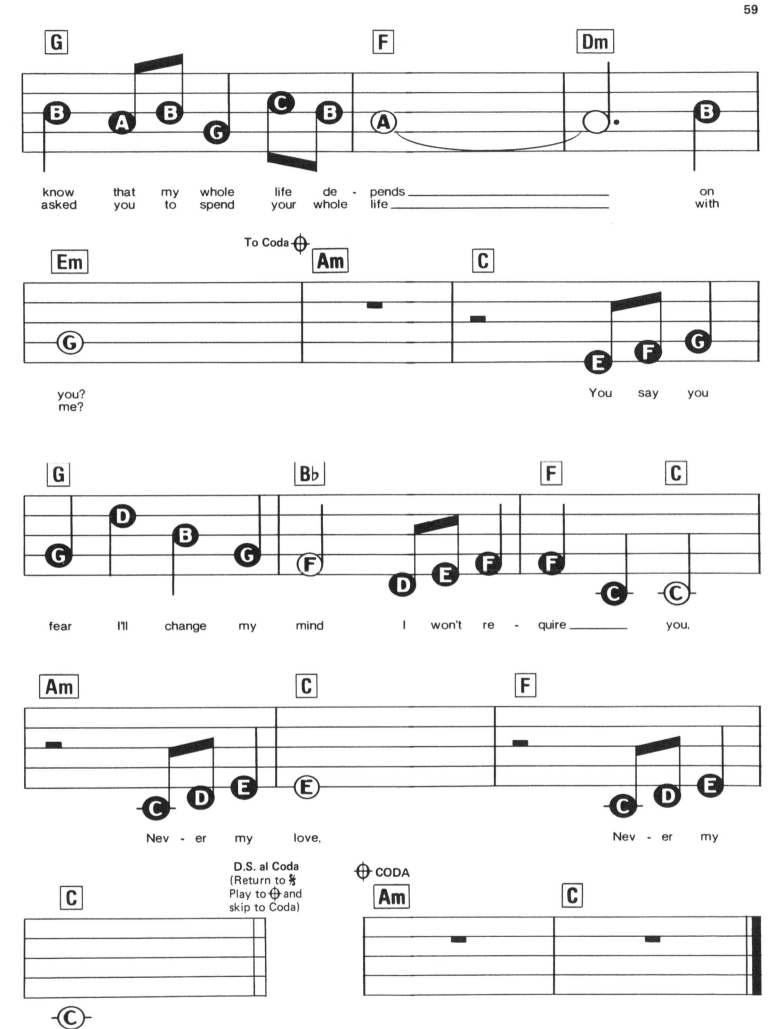

On Broadway

Registration 7
Rhythm: Rock

Words and Music by Barry Mann,
Cynthia Weil, Mike Stoller
and Jerry Leiber

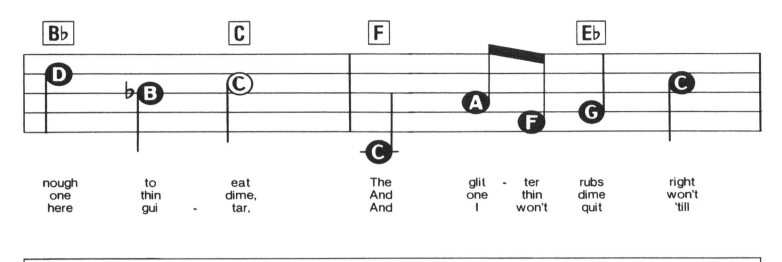

nough to eat The glit - ter rubs right
one thin dime, And one thin dime won't
here gui - tar, And I won't quit 'till

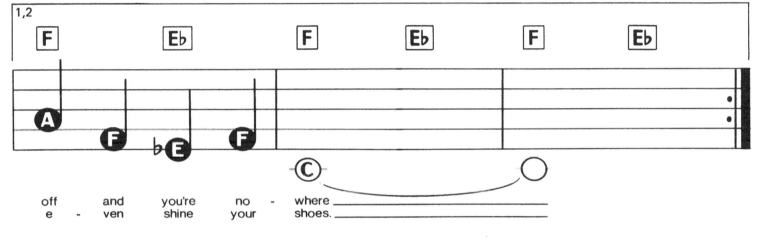

off and you're no - where _____
e - ven shine your shoes. _____

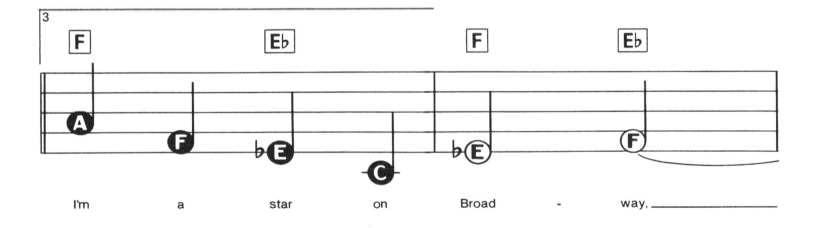

I'm a star on Broad - way, _____

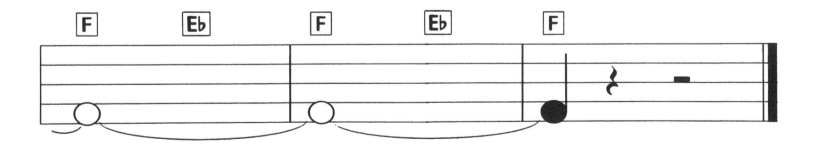

Rhinestone Cowboy

Registration 4
Rhythm: Country or Shuffle

Words and Music by Larry Weiss

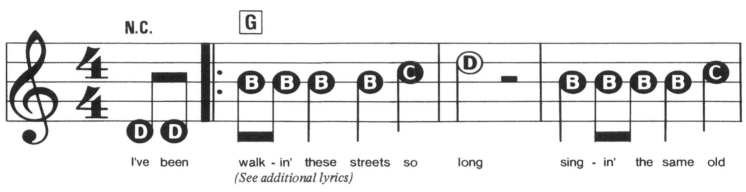

I've been walk - in' these streets so long sing - in' the same old
(See additional lyrics)

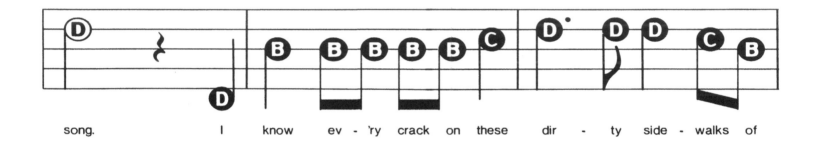

song. I know ev - 'ry crack on these dir - ty side - walks of

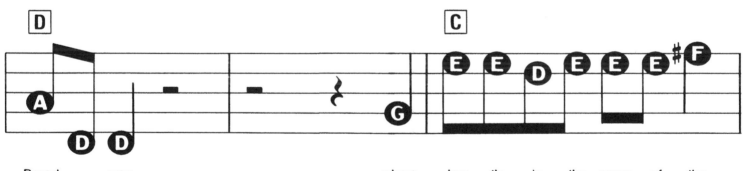

Broad - way, where hus - tle is the name of the

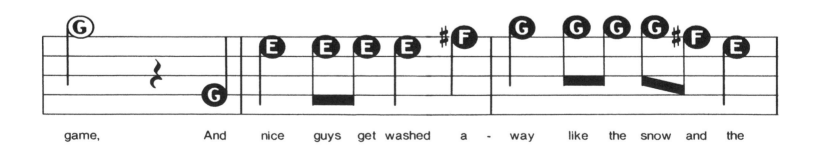

game, And nice guys get washed a - way like the snow and the

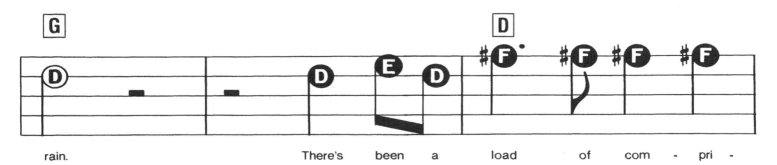

rain.   There's been a load of com - pri -

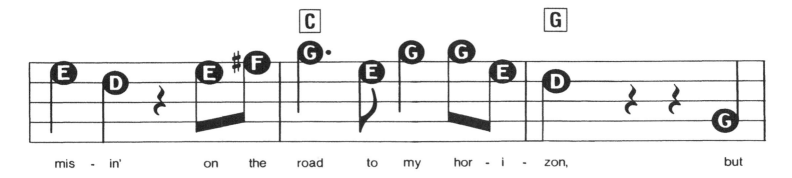

mis - in' on the road to my hor - i - zon, but

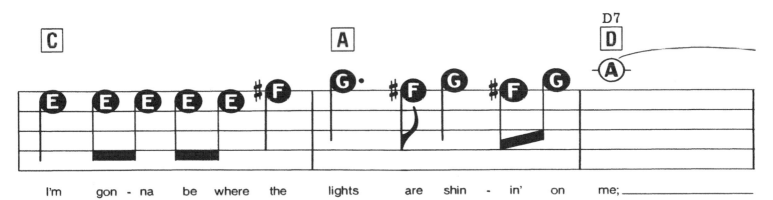

I'm gon - na be where the lights are shin - in' on me;____

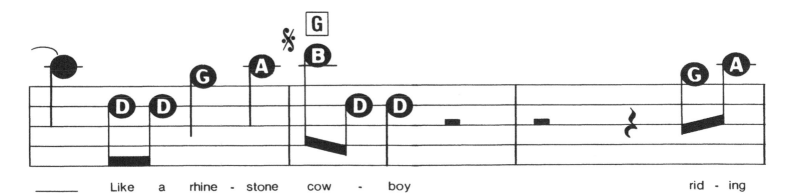

____ Like a rhine - stone cow - boy riding

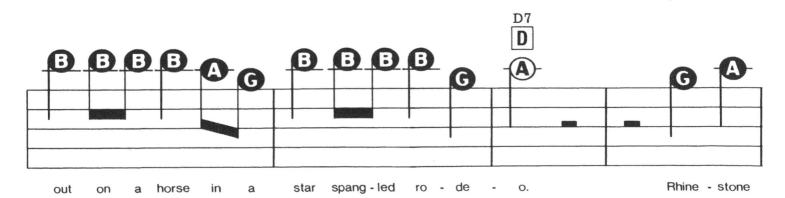

out on a horse in a star spang - led ro - de - o.   Rhine - stone

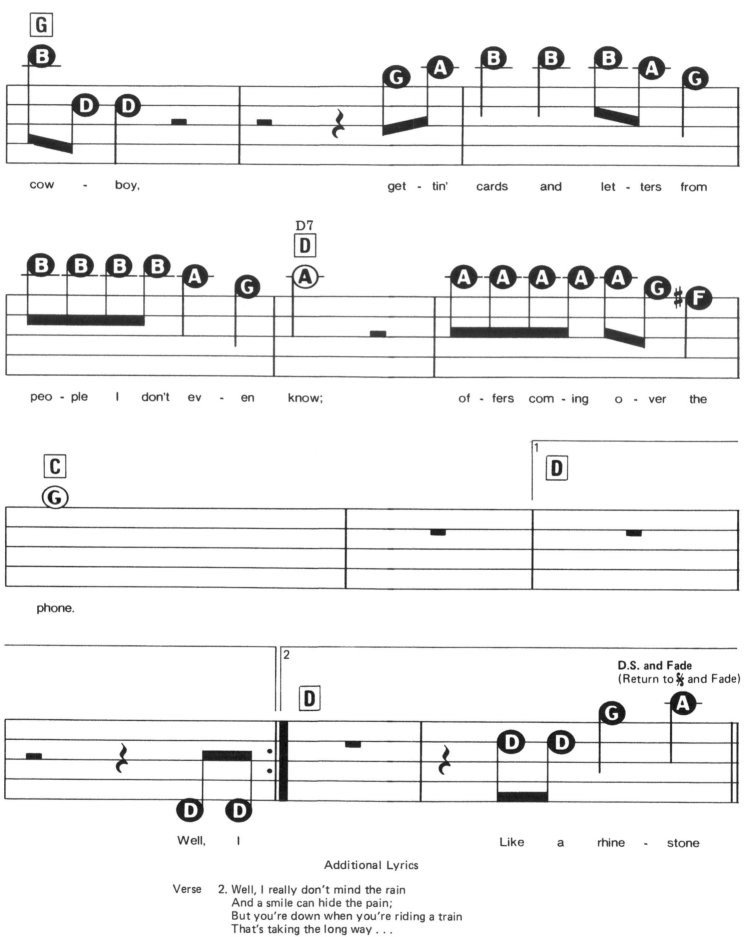

cow - boy, get - tin' cards and let - ters from

peo - ple I don't ev - en know; of - fers com - ing o - ver the

phone.

Well, I Like a rhine - stone

Additional Lyrics

Verse 2. Well, I really don't mind the rain
And a smile can hide the pain;
But you're down when you're riding a train
That's taking the long way . . .
But I dream of the things I'll do
With a subway token and a dollar
Tucked inside my shoe . . .
There's been a load of compromisin'
On the road to my horizon;
But I'm gonna be where the lights are shinin' on me . . .
(Like a) . . . (to Chorus and fade)

The Rose

(From the Twentieth Century-Fox Motion Picture Release "THE ROSE")

Registration 5
Rhythm: Rock or Slow Rock

Words and Music by Amanda McBroom

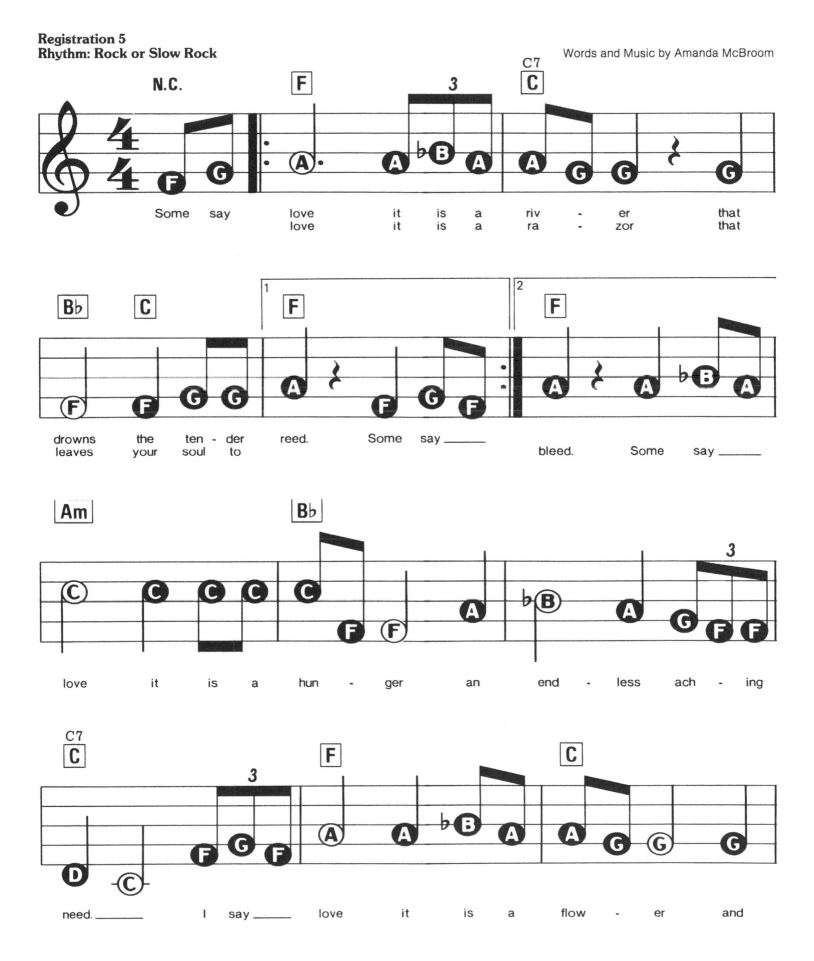

66

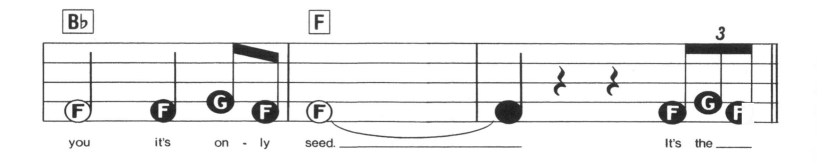

you   it's   on - ly   seed. _____   It's   the _____

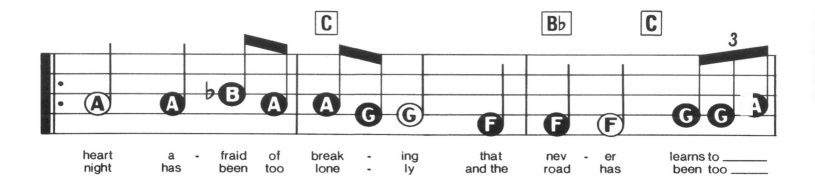

heart   a - fraid   of   break - ing   that   nev - er   learns to _____
night   has   been   too   lone - ly   and the   road   has   been too _____

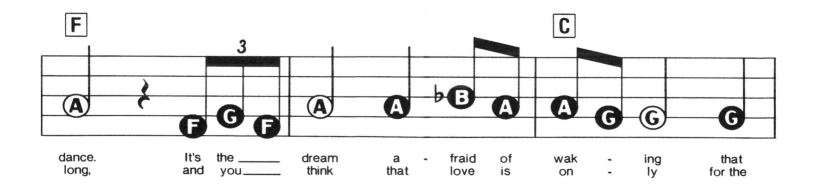

dance.   It's   the _____ dream   a - fraid   of   wak - ing   that
long,   and   you _____ think   that   love   is   on - ly   for the

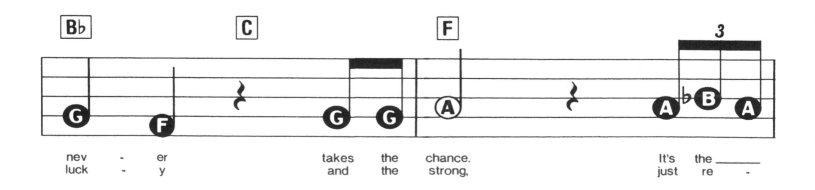

nev - er   takes   the   chance.   It's   the _____
luck - y   and   the   strong,   just   re -

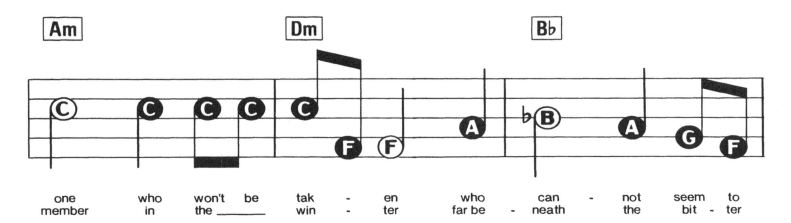

one who won't be tak - en who can - not seem to
member in the _____ win - ter far be - neath the bit - ter

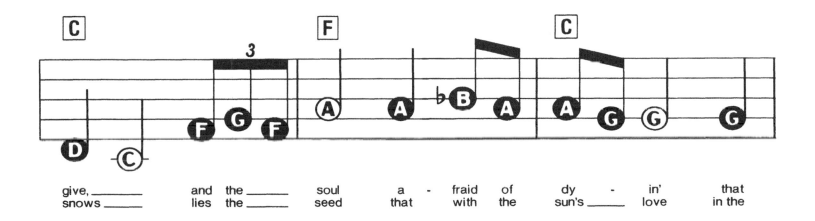

give, _____ and the _____ soul a - fraid of dy - in' that
snows _____ lies the _____ seed that with the sun's _____ love in the

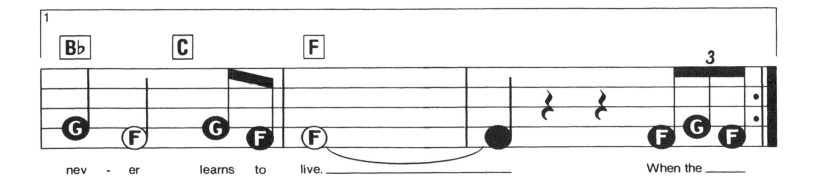

nev - er learns to live. _____ When the _____

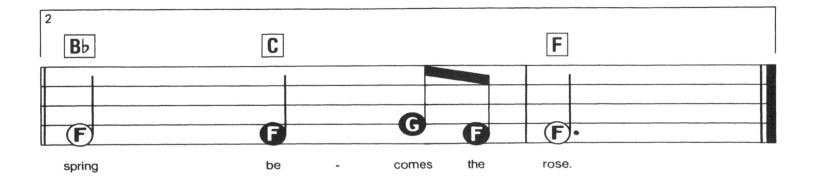

spring be - comes the rose.

Southern Cross

Registration 1
Rhythm: Rock or Slow Rock

Words and Music by Stephen Stills,
Richard Curtis and Michael Curtis

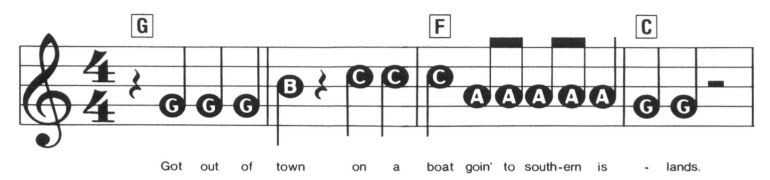

Got out of town on a boat goin' to south-ern is - lands.

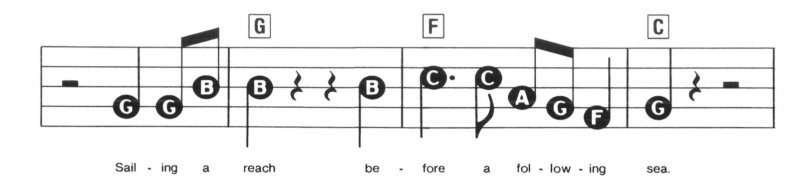

Sail - ing a reach be - fore a fol - low - ing sea.

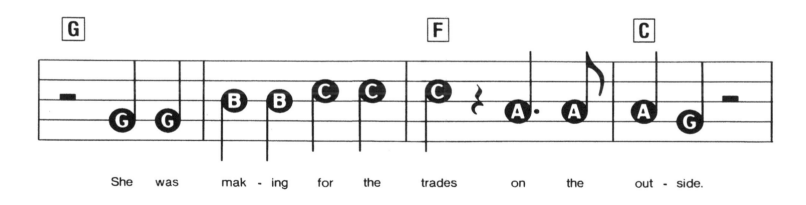

She was mak - ing for the trades on the out - side.

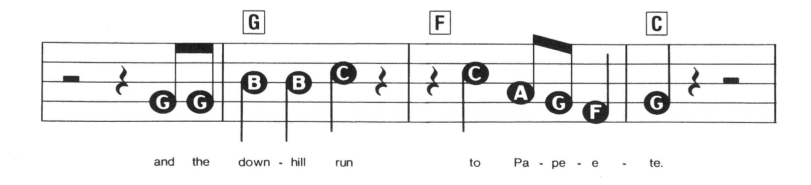

and the down - hill run to Pa - pe - e - te.

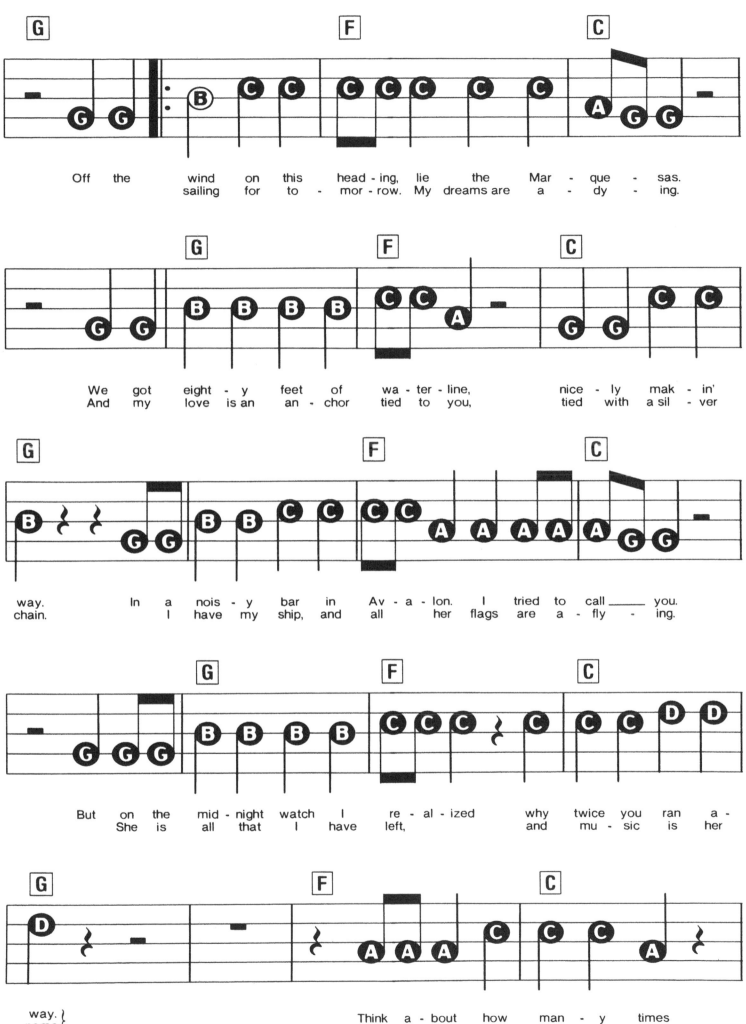

70

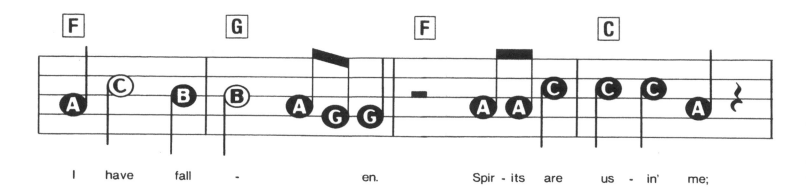

I have fall - en. Spir - its are us - in' me;

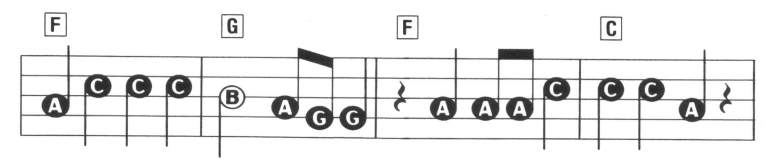

larg - er voic - es call - in'. What heav - en brought you and me

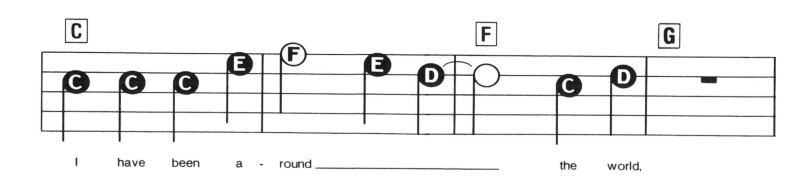

can - not be for - got - ten.

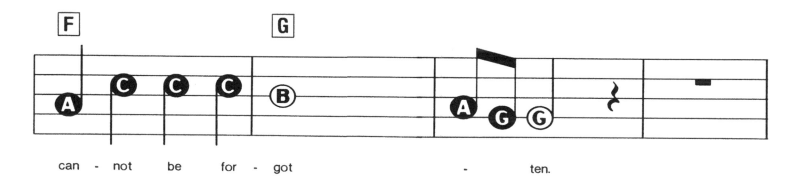

I have been a - round _____ the world,

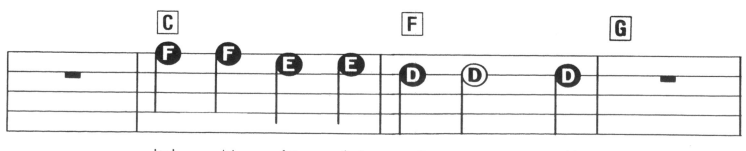

look - in' for that wom - an - girl

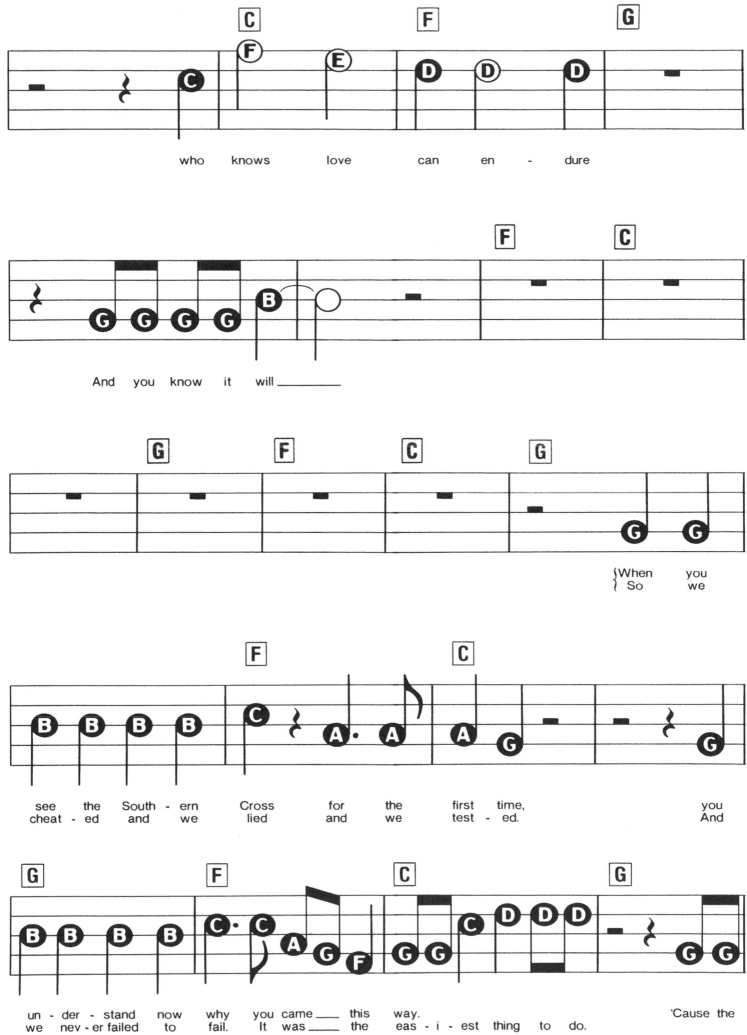

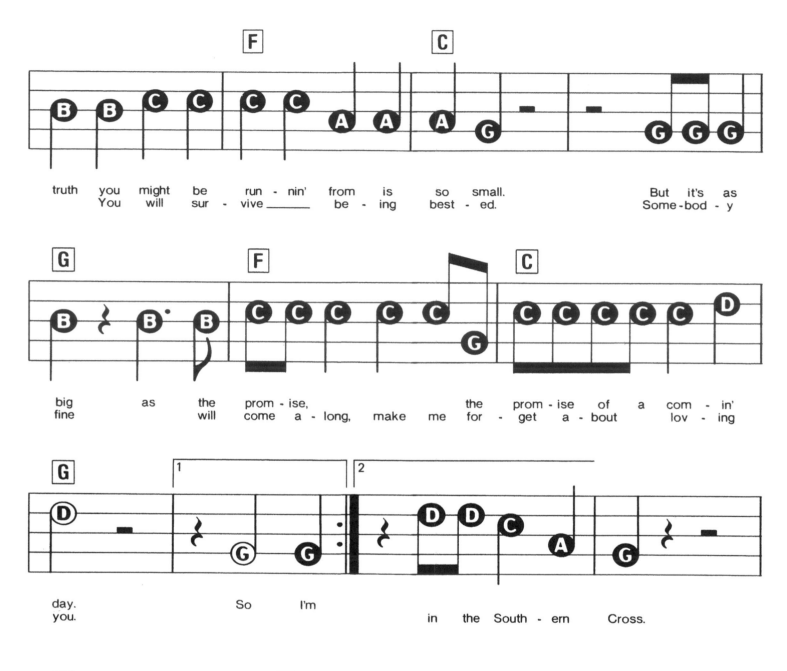

truth you might be run - nin' from is so small. But it's as
You will sur - vive _____ be - ing best - ed. Some-bod - y

big as the prom - ise, the prom - ise of a com - in'
fine will come a - long, make me for - get a - bout lov - ing

day. So I'm
you. in the South - ern Cross.

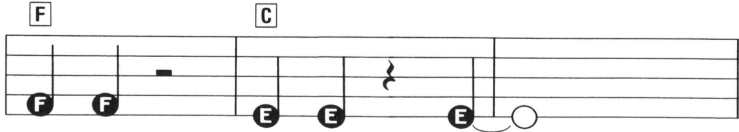

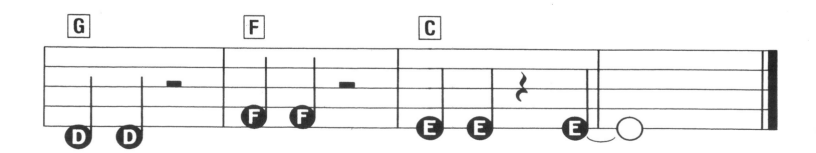

Southern Nights

Words and Music by
Allan Toussaint

Registration 10
Rhythm: Rock or Slow Rock

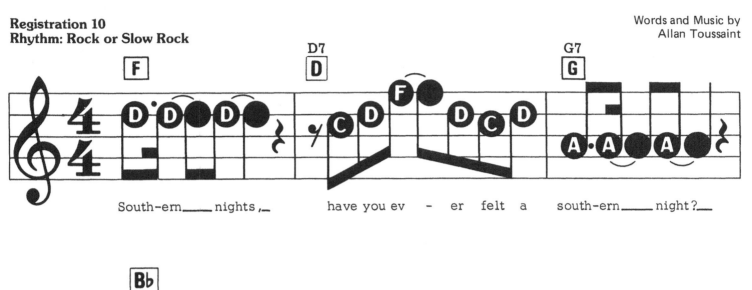

South-ern___ nights,___ have you ev – er felt a south-ern___ night?___

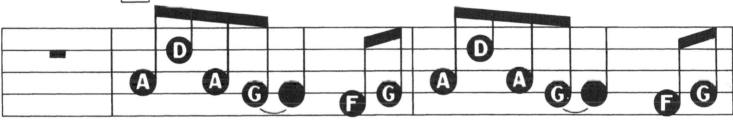

Free as a breeze,___ not to men-tion the trees,___ whis-tling

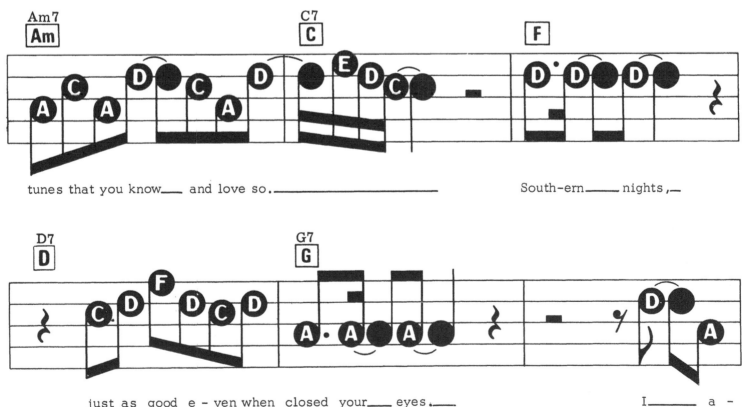

tunes that you know___ and love so._____ South-ern___ nights,___

just as good e - ven when closed your___ eyes.___ I___ a -

74

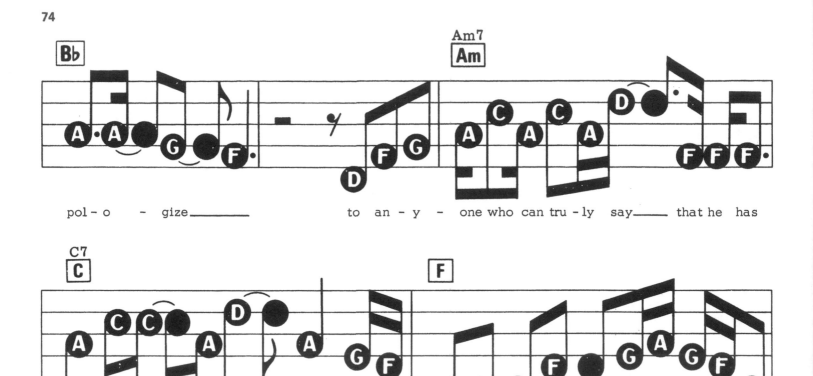

pol - o - gize_____ to an - y - one who can tru -ly say_____ that he has

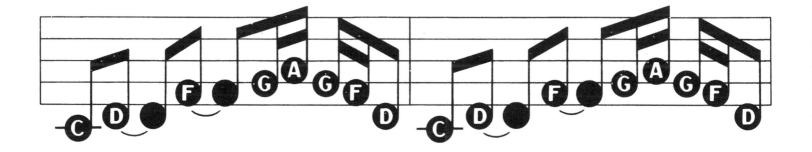

found a bet - ter way._____

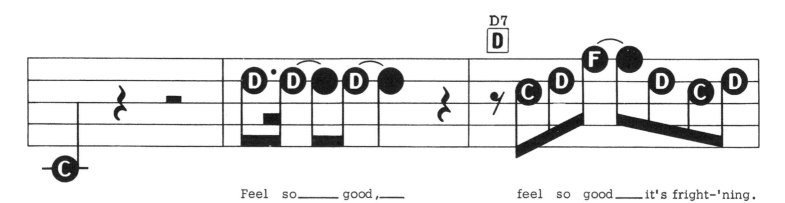

Feel so_____ good,_____ feel so good_____it's fright-'ning.

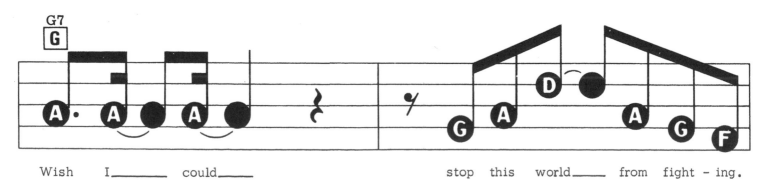

Wish I_____ could_____ stop this world_____ from fight - ing.

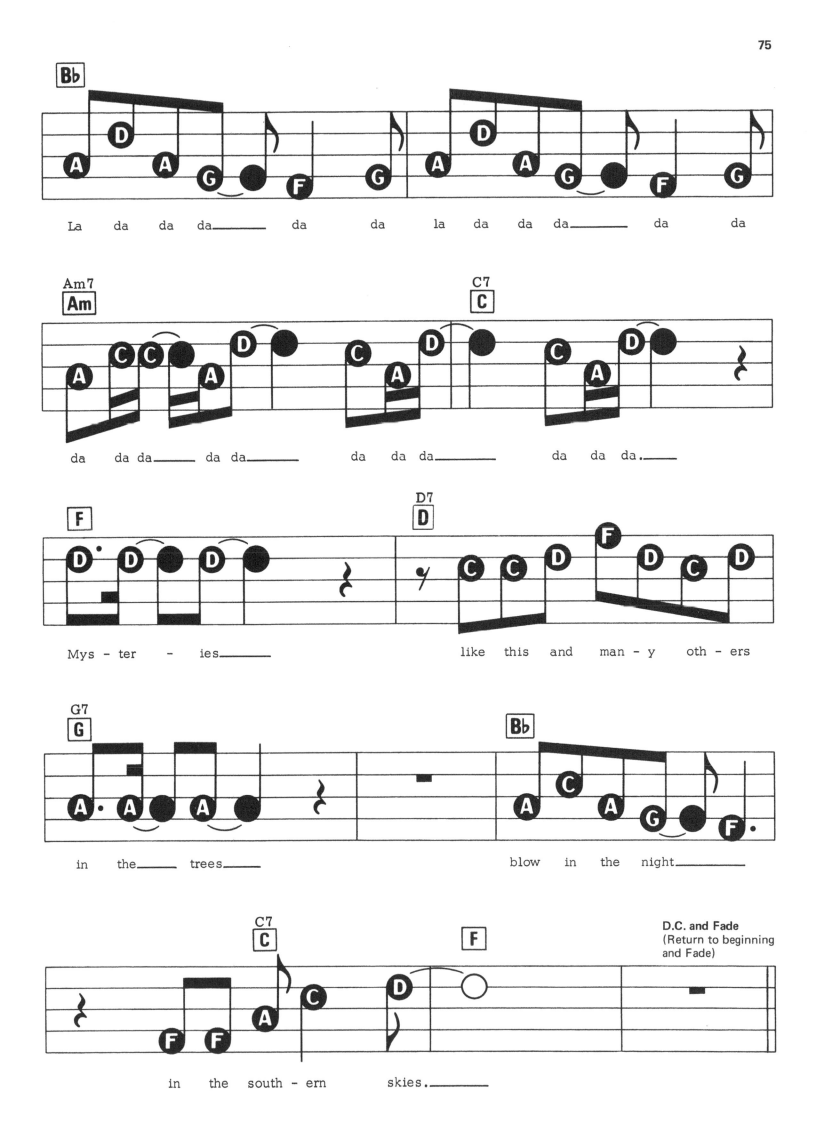

(Main Theme)
Star Wars

(From the Motion Picture "STAR WARS" & "THE EMPIRE STRIKES BACK"
A Lucasfilm Ltd. Production — A Twentieth Century - Fox Release)

Registration 5
Rhythm: March

Music by John Williams

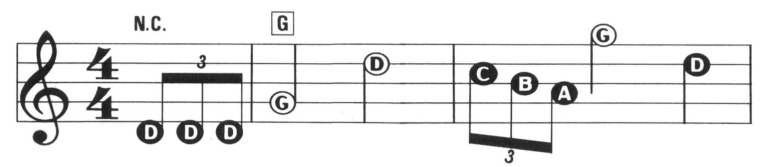

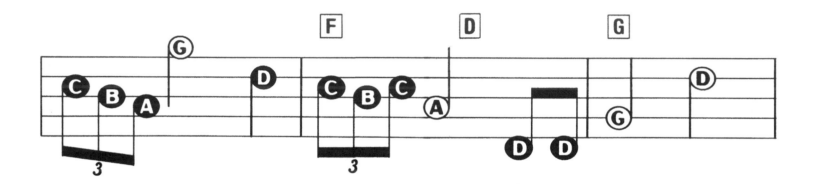

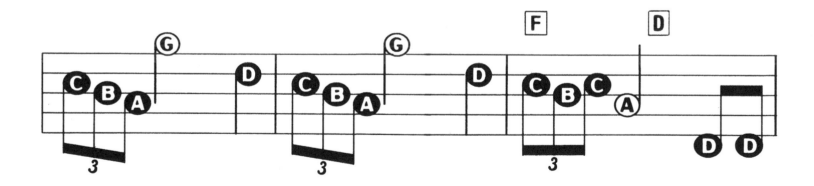

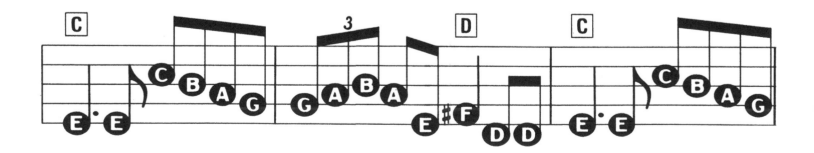

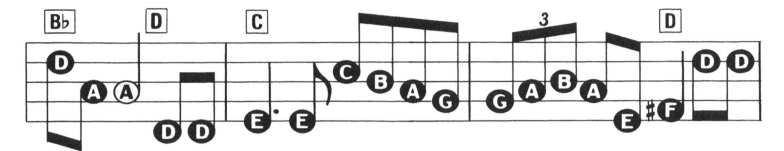

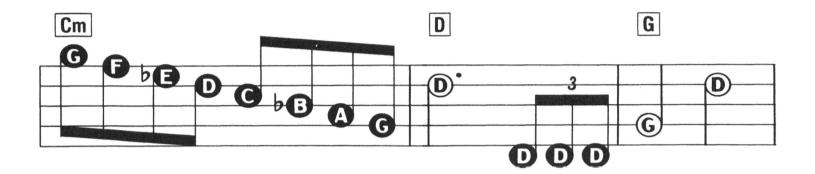

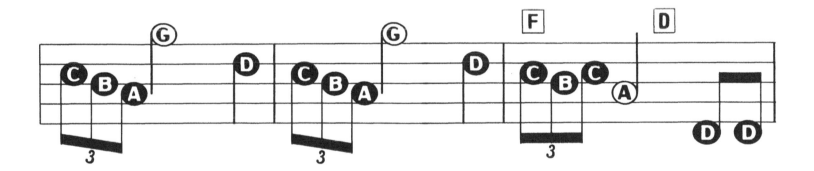

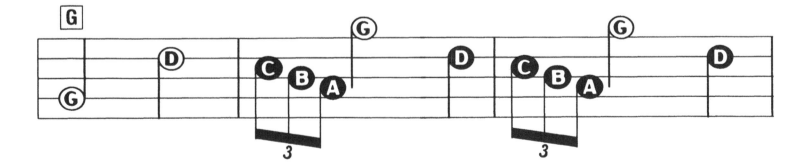

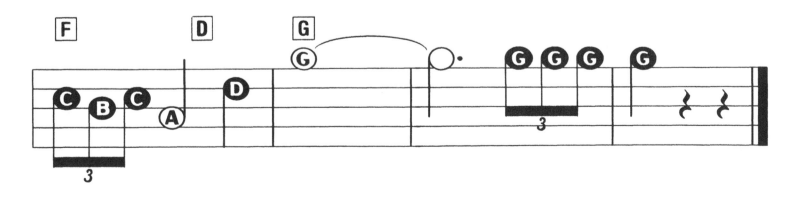

(Slow Dancin')
Swayin' To The Music

Registration 2
Rhythm: Slow Rock or Ballad

Words and Music by Jack Tempchin

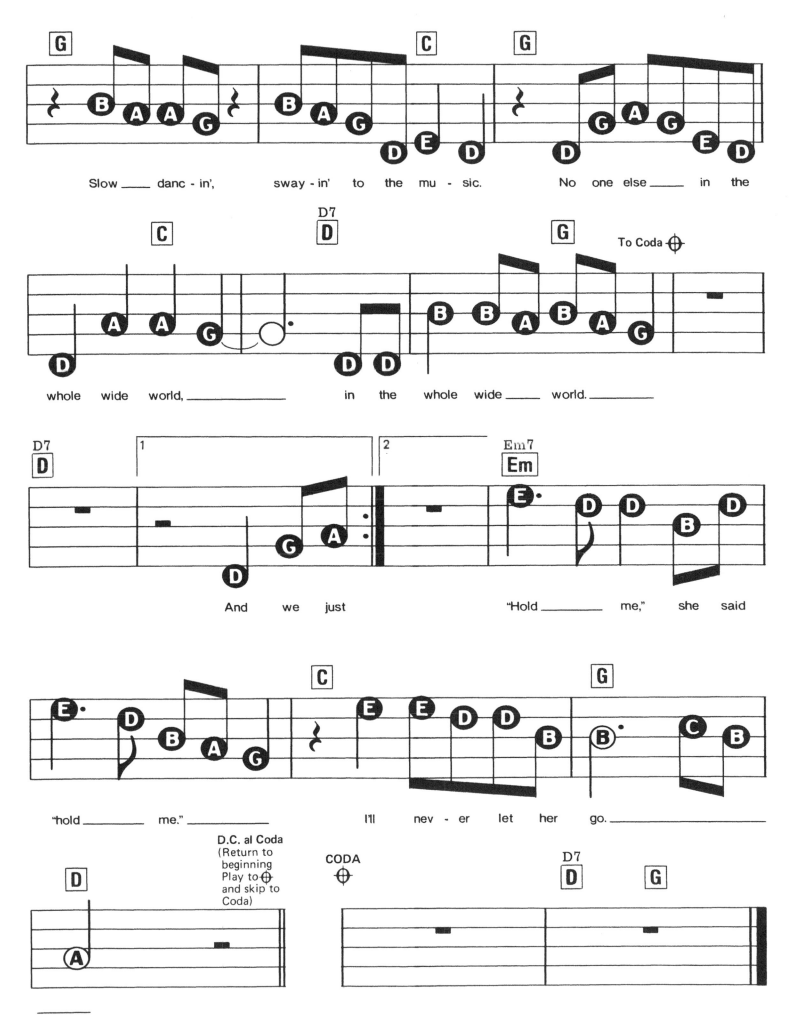

Take It To The Limit

Registration 3
Rhythm: Waltz

Words and Music by Randy Meisner, Don Henley and Glenn Frey

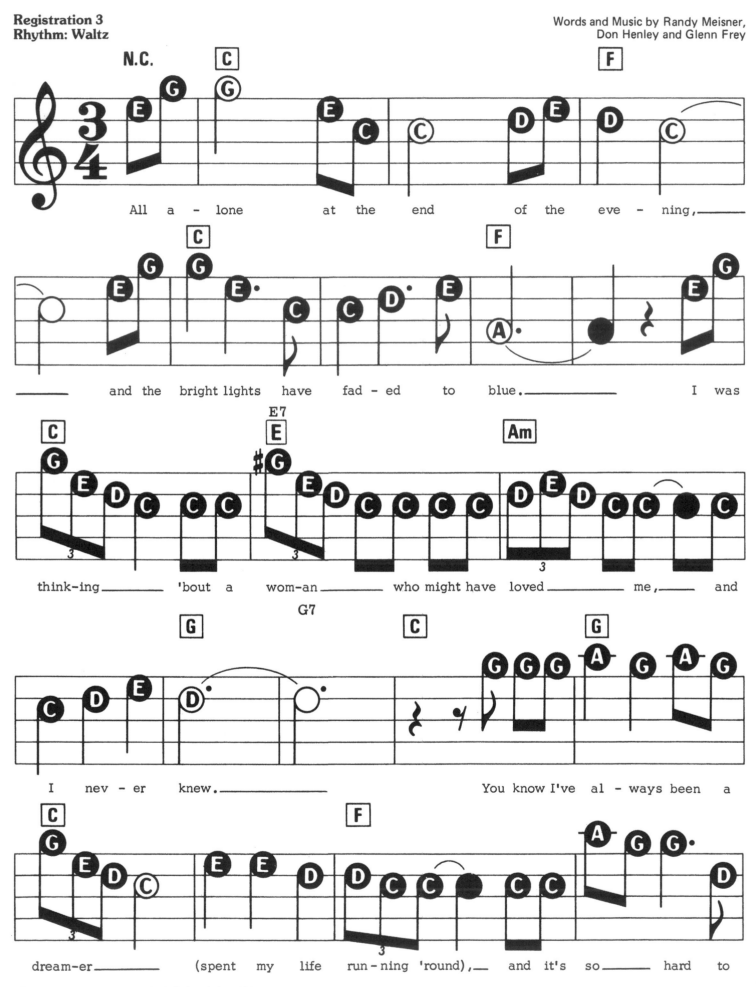

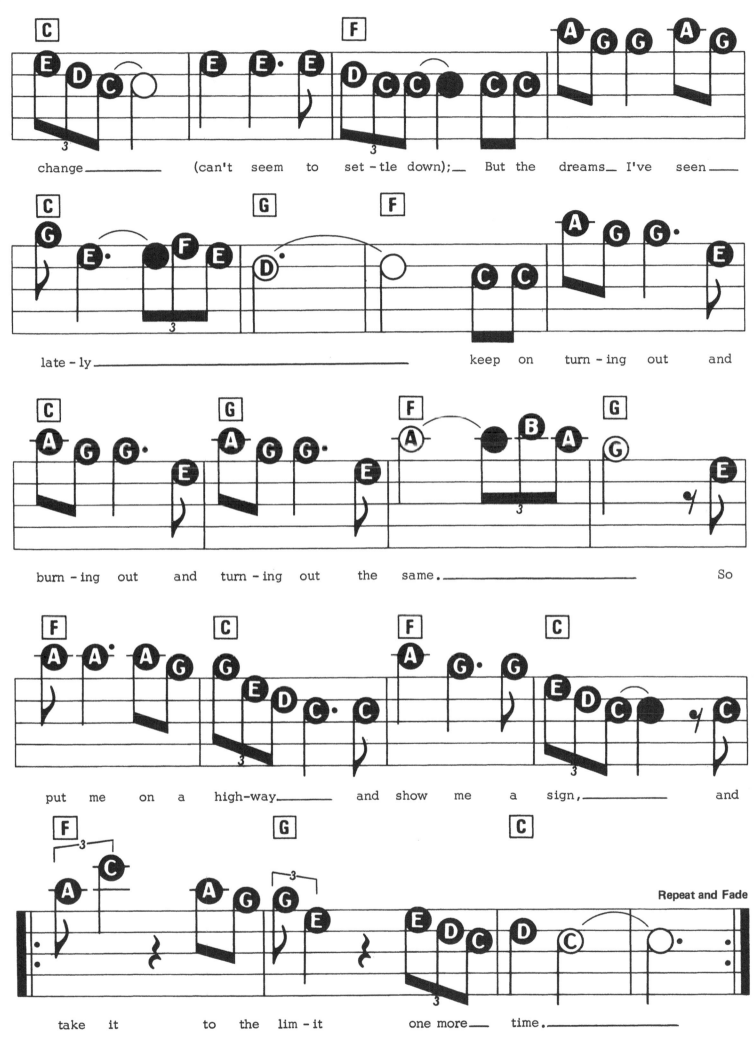

Time In A Bottle

Registration 8
Rhythm: Waltz

Words and Music by
Jim Croce

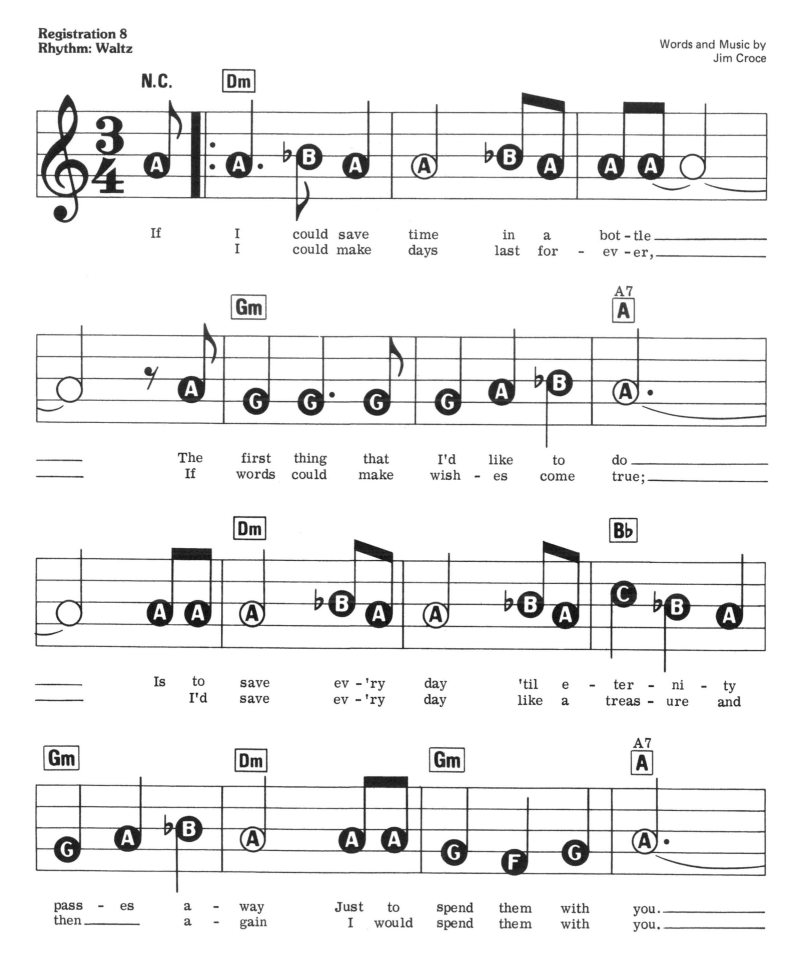

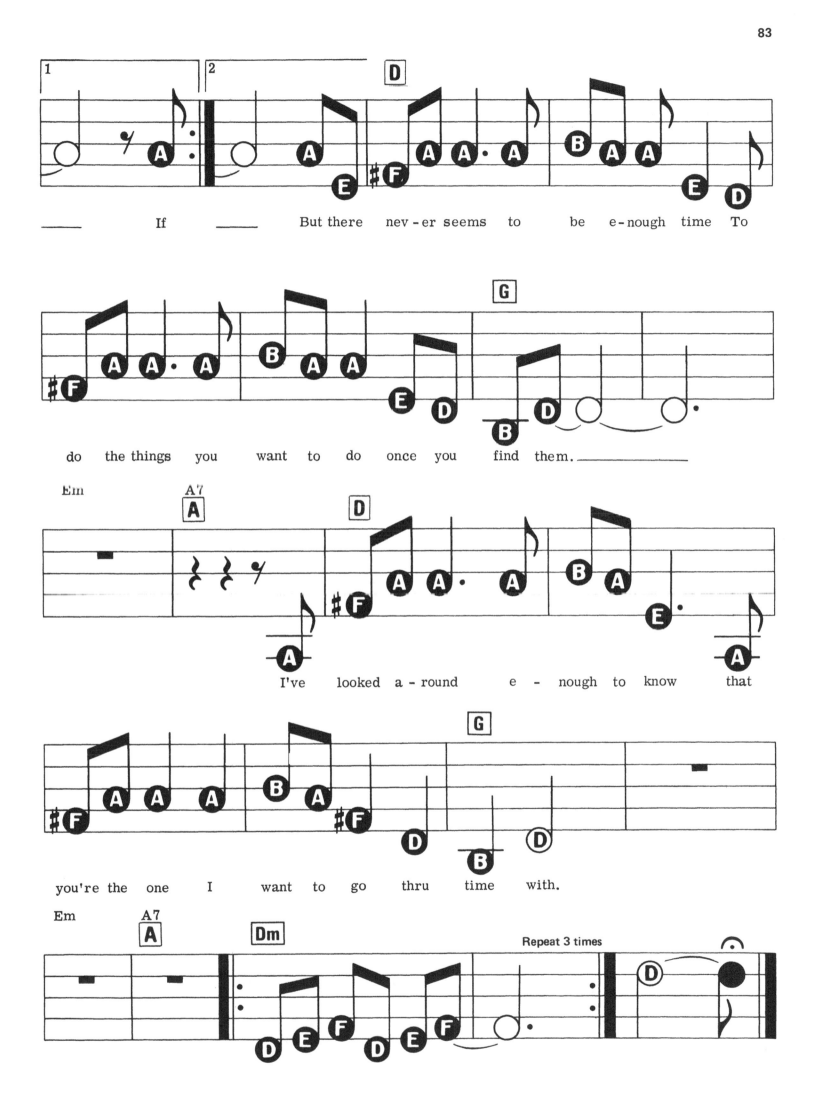

Tin Man

Registration 4
Rhythm: Rock or Slow Rock

Words and Music by
Dewey Bunnell

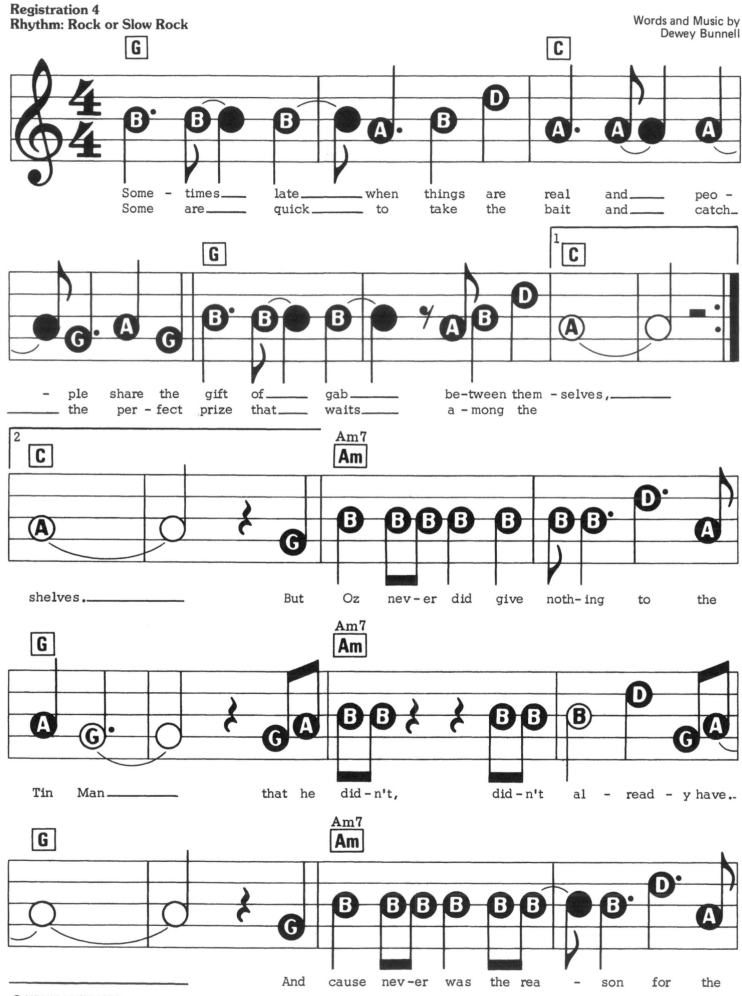

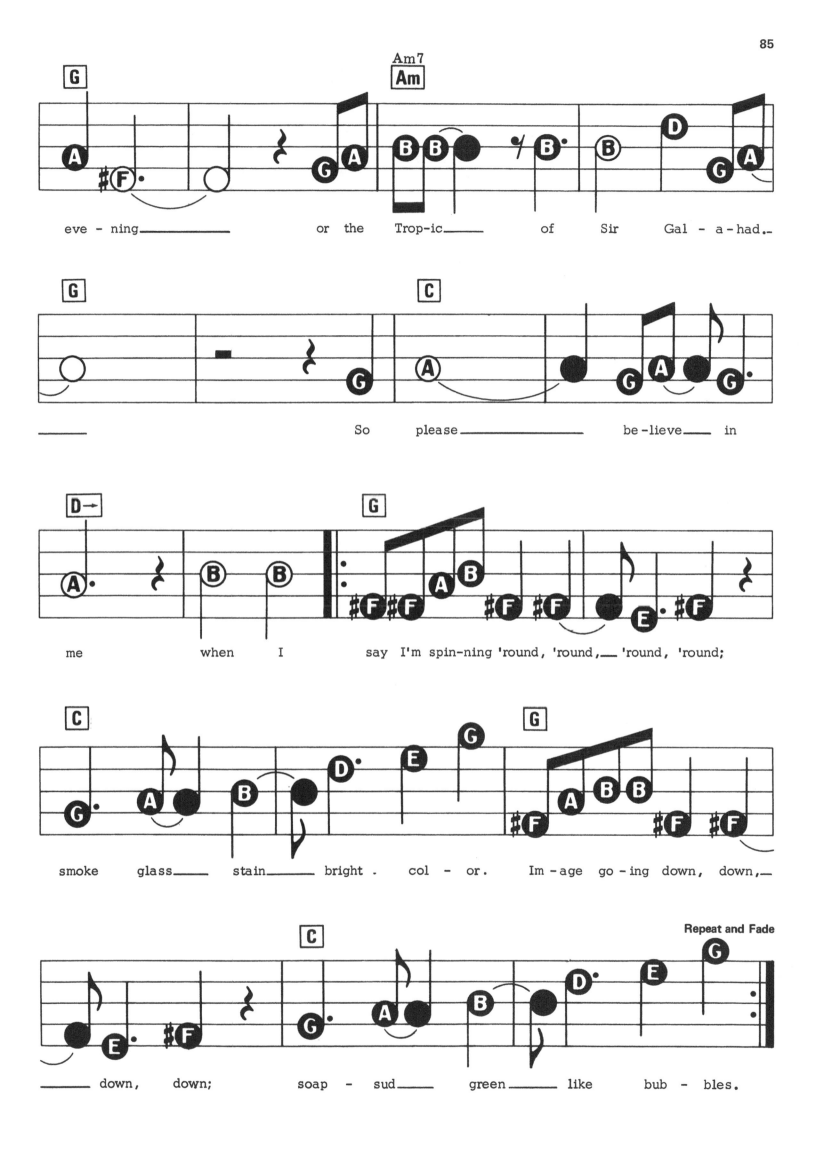

Too Much, Too Little, Too Late

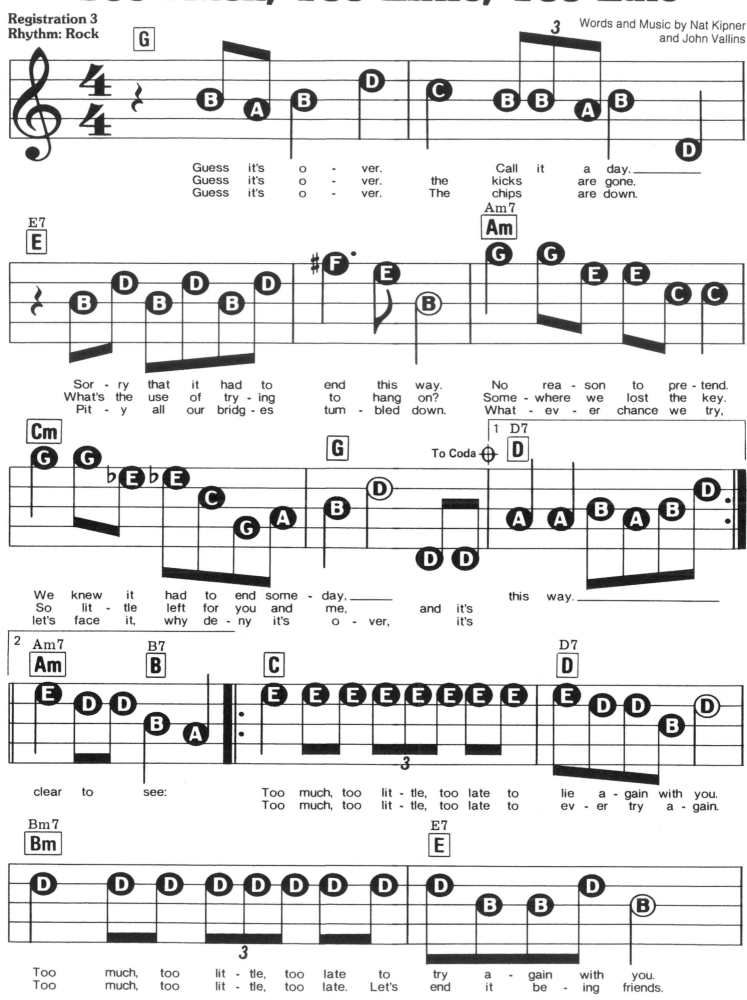

Registration 3
Rhythm: Rock

Words and Music by Nat Kipner
and John Vallins

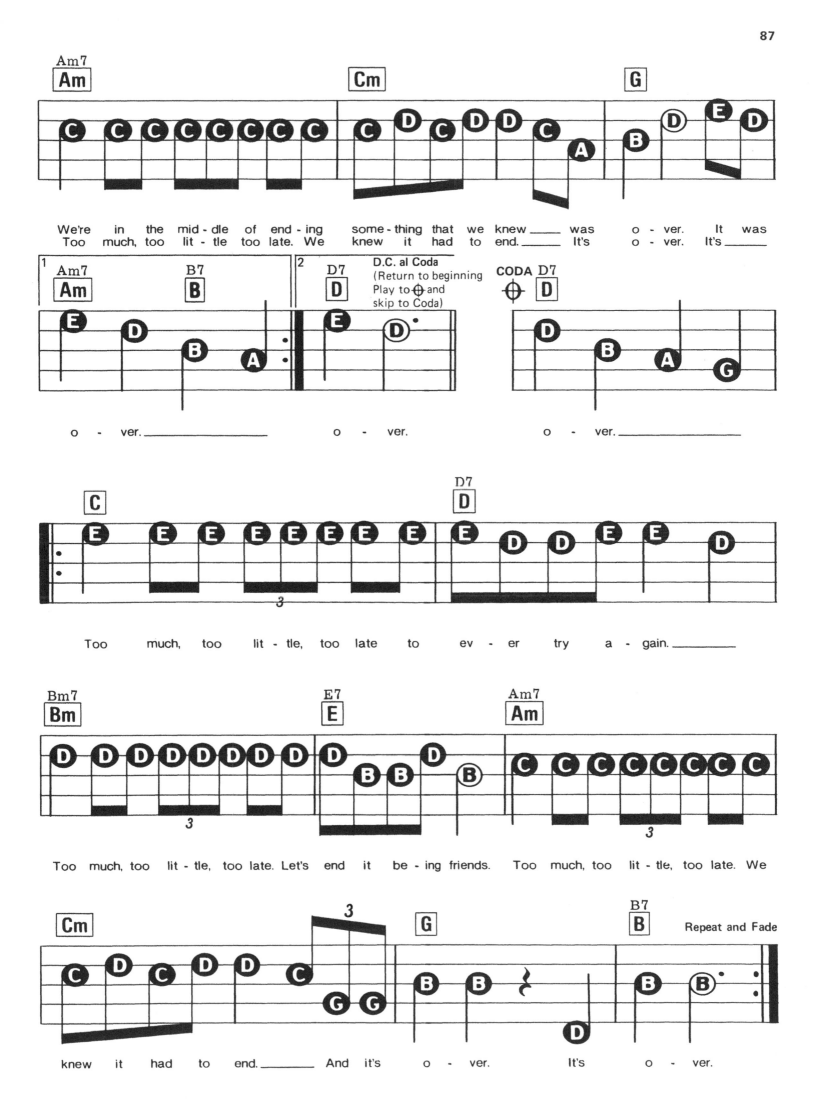

Sundown

Registration 10
Rhythm: Rock or Slow Rock

Words and Music by
Gordon Lightfoot

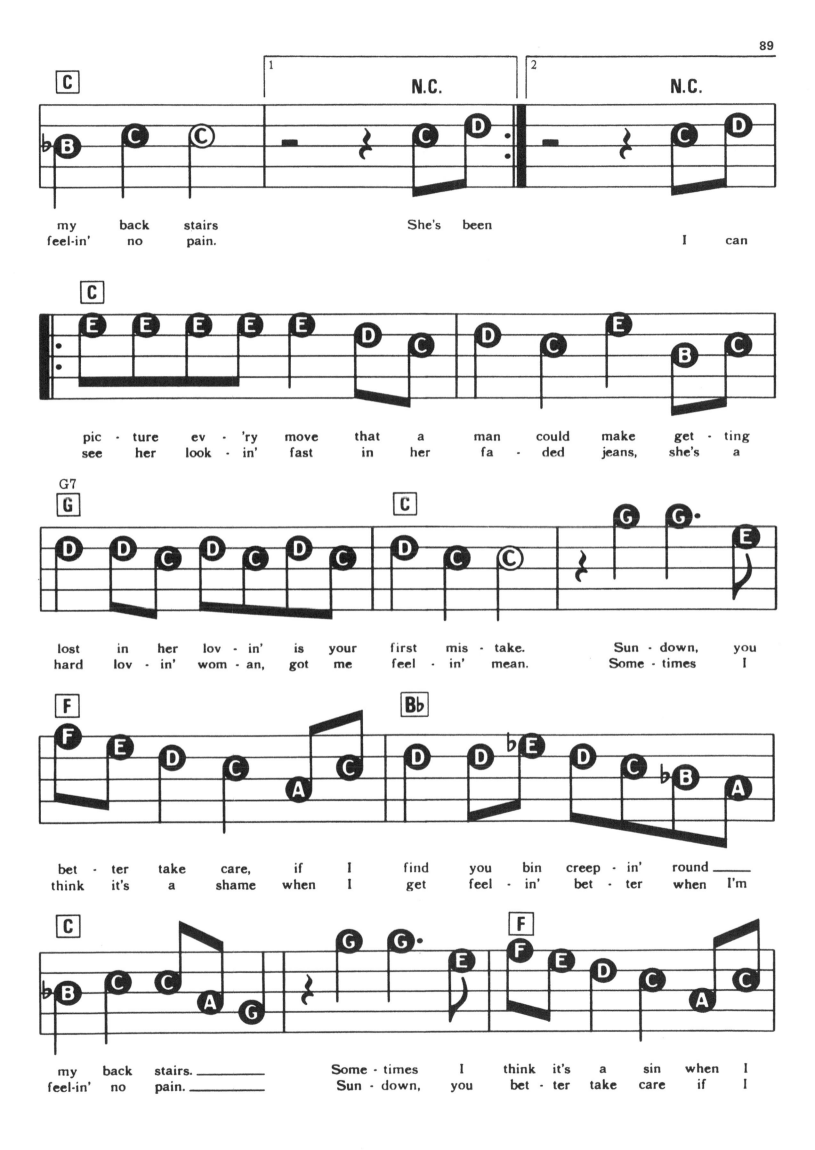

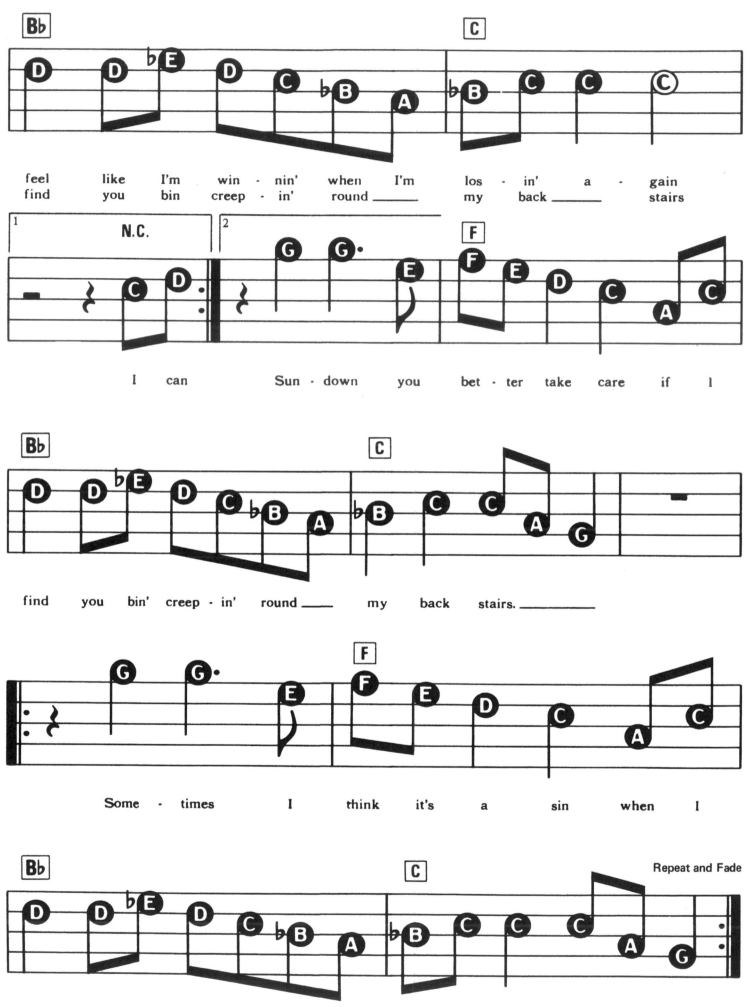

Ventura Highway

Registration 9
Rhythm: Rock or Disco

Words and Music by Dewey Bunnell

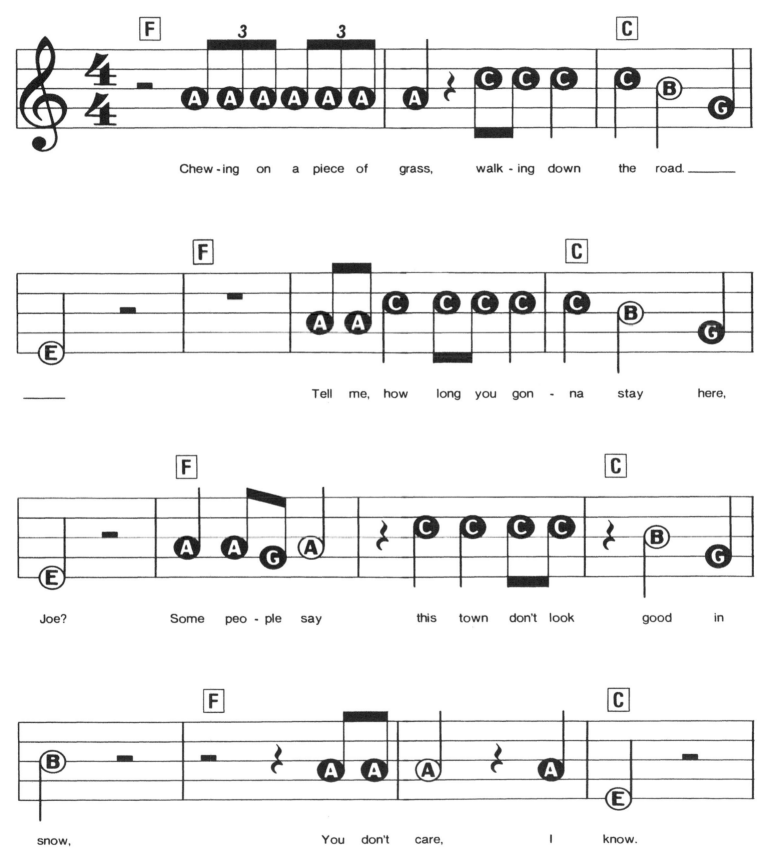

Chew-ing on a piece of grass, walk-ing down the road. _____

_____ Tell me, how long you gon-na stay here,

Joe? Some peo-ple say this town don't look good in

snow, You don't care, I know.

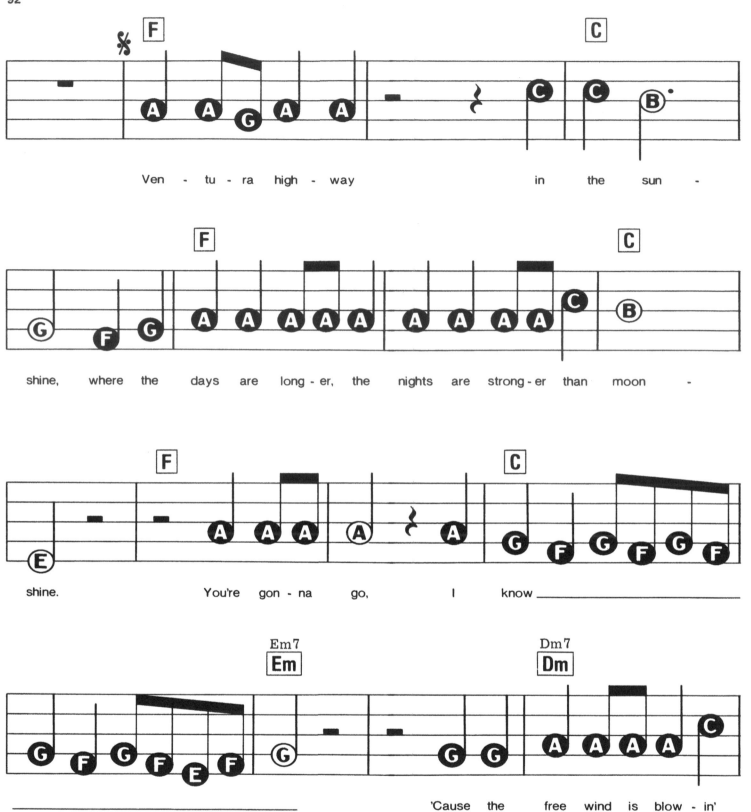

Ven - tu - ra high - way   in the sun -

shine, where the days are long - er, the nights are strong - er than moon -

shine.   You're gon - na go, I know

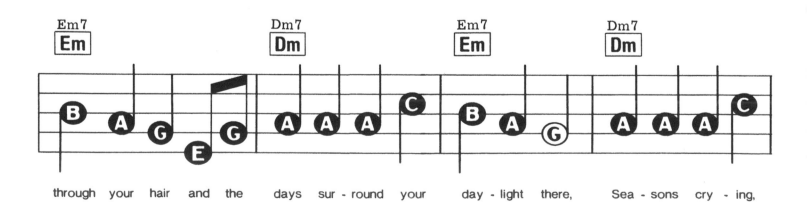

'Cause the free wind is blow - in'

through your hair and the days sur - round your day - light there, Sea - sons cry - ing,

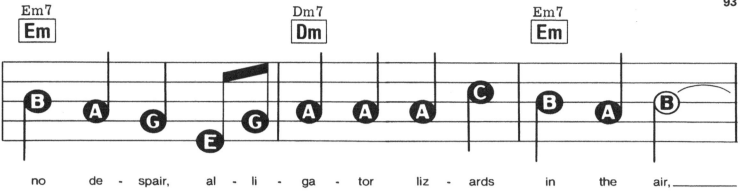

no de - spair, al - li - ga - tor liz - ards in the air, _____

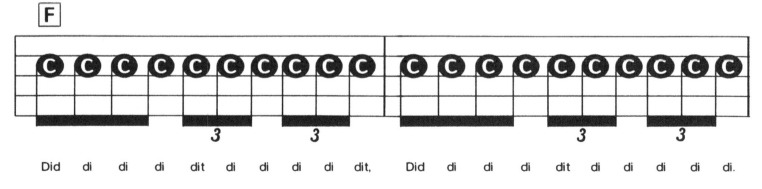

To Coda ⊕

_____ in the air, _____

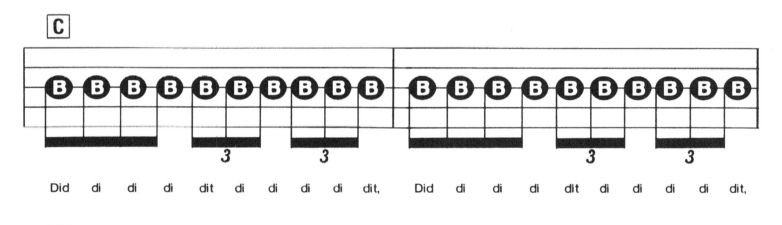

Did di di di dit di di di di dit, Did di di di dit di di di di dit,

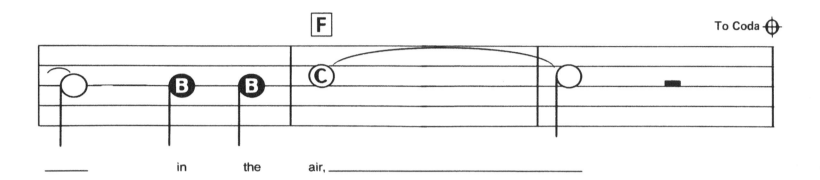

Did di di di dit di di di di dit, Did di di di dit di di di di di.

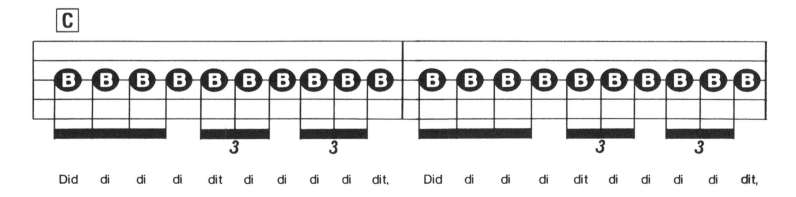

Did di di di dit di di di di dit, Did di di di dit di di di di dit,

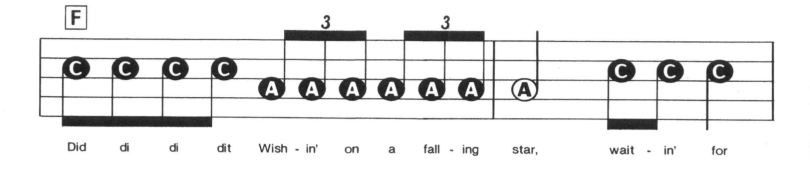

Did di di dit Wish - in' on a fall - ing star, wait - in' for

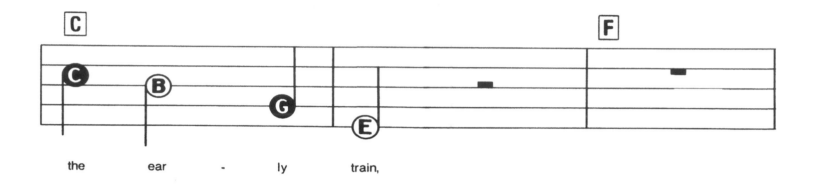

the ear - ly train,

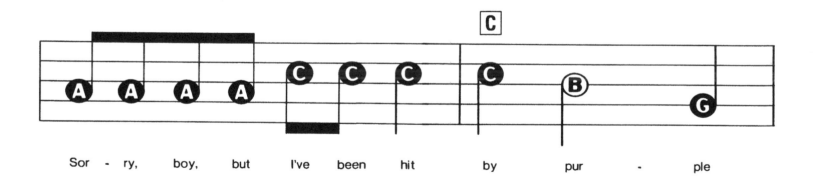

Sor - ry, boy, but I've been hit by pur - ple

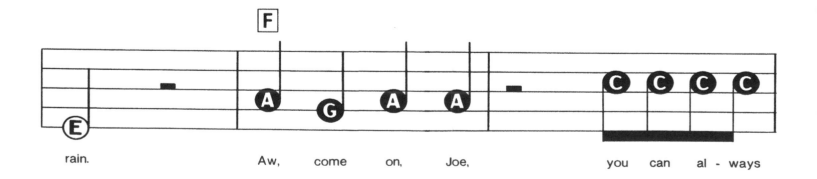

rain. Aw, come on, Joe, you can al - ways

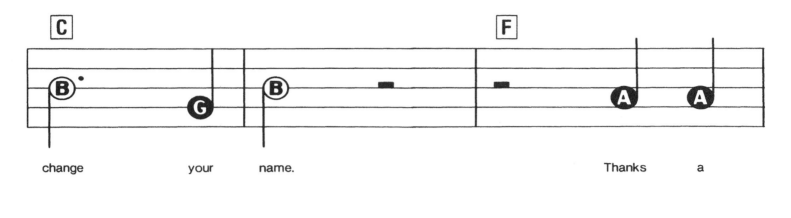

change   your   name.   Thanks   a

D.S. al Coda
(Return to 𝄉
Play to ⊕ and
skip to Coda)

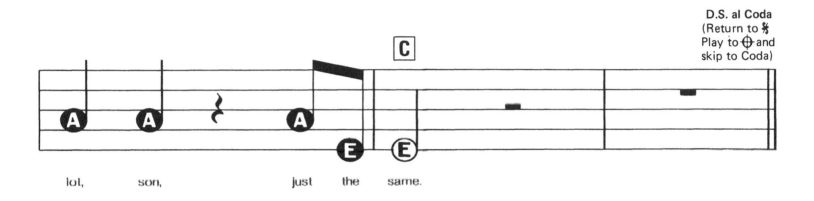

lot,   son,   just   the   same.

CODA
⊕

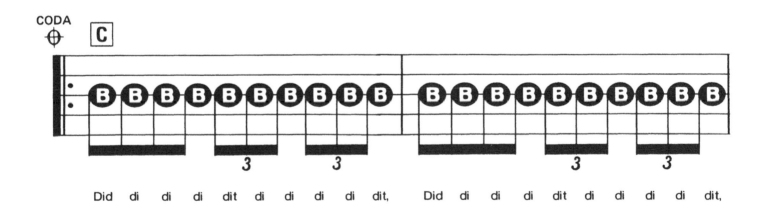

Did   di   di   di   dit   di   di   di   di   dit,   Did   di   di   di   dit   di   di   di   di   dit,

Repeat and Fade

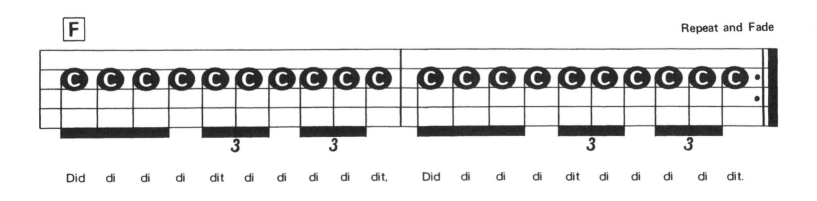

Did   di   di   di   dit   di   di   di   di   dit,   Did   di   di   di   dit   di   di   di   di   dit.

We Are Family

Registration 2
Rhythm: Rock or Jazz Rock

*The rests which appear in the Repeat and Fade ending
(last 8 measures of the song) make it possible to reduce
the volume in two different ways:*
  1) by changing the registration to a softer sound.
  2) by using the Expression pedal.

Words and Music by
Nile Rodgers and Bernard Edwards

We are fam - i - ly.   I got all my sis - ters with me.

We are fam - i - ly.

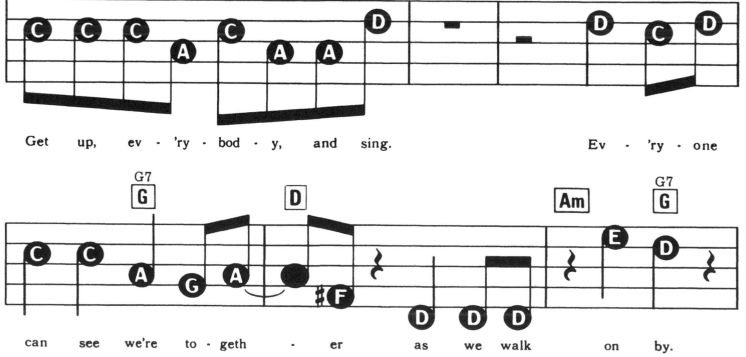

Get up, ev - 'ry - bod - y, and sing.   Ev - 'ry - one

can see we're to - geth - er as we walk on by.

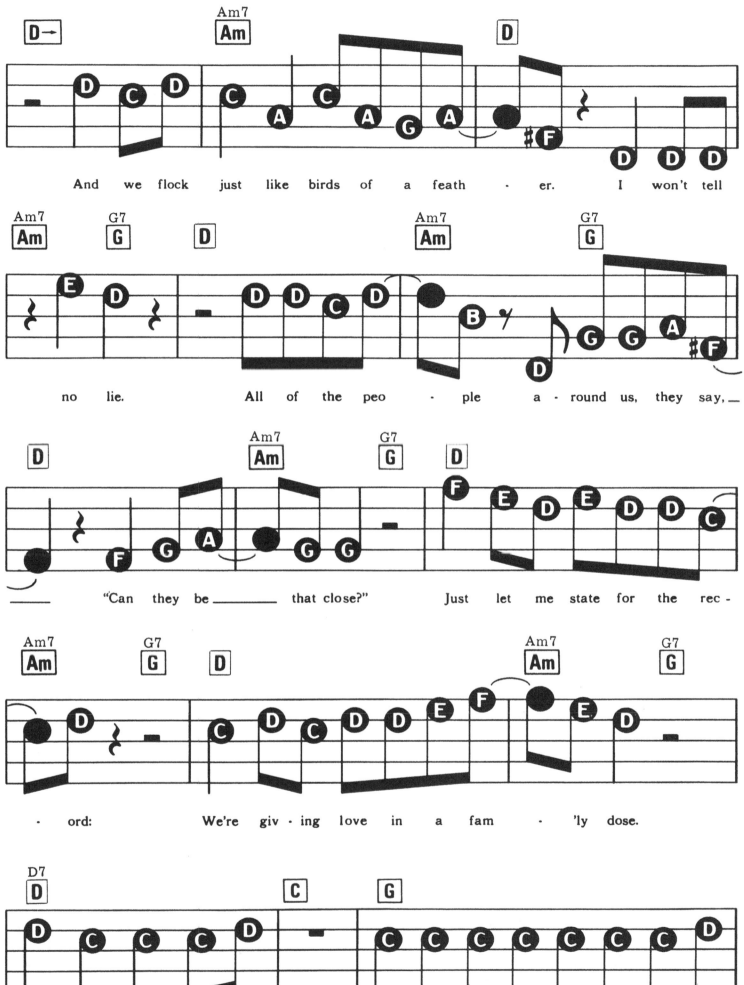

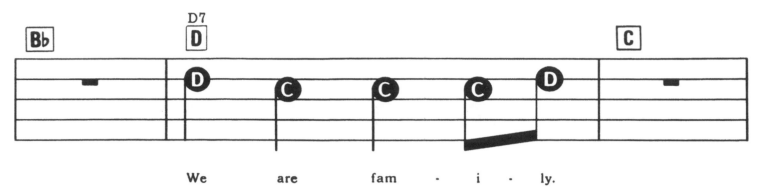

We are fam - i - ly.

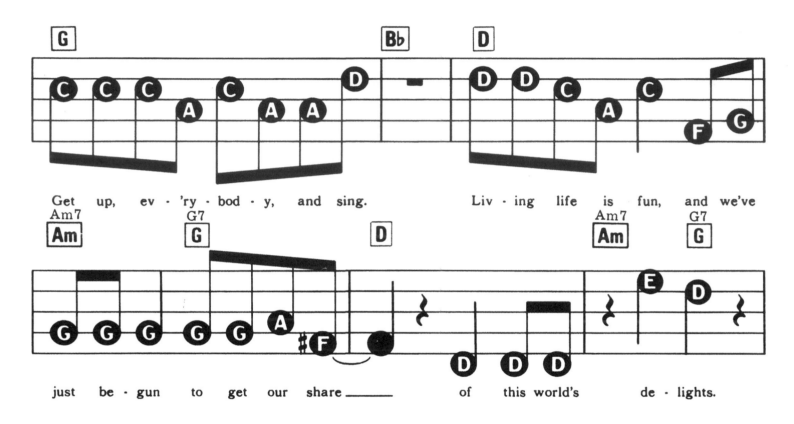

Get up, ev - 'ry - bod - y, and sing.   Liv - ing life is fun, and we've

just be - gun to get our share _____ of this world's de - lights.

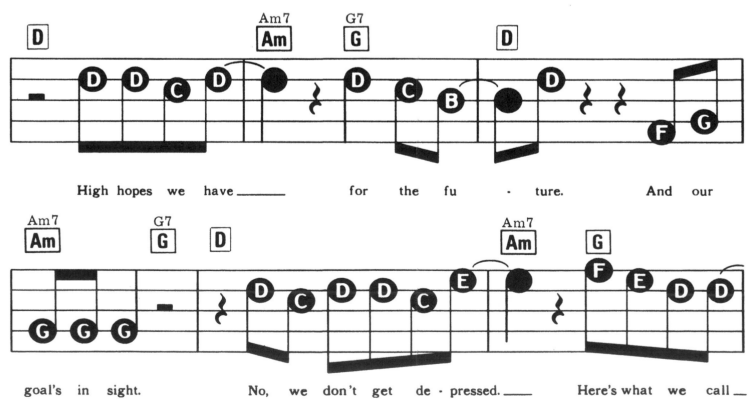

High hopes we have _____ for the fu - ture.   And our

goal's in sight.   No, we don't get de - pressed. ____ Here's what we call __

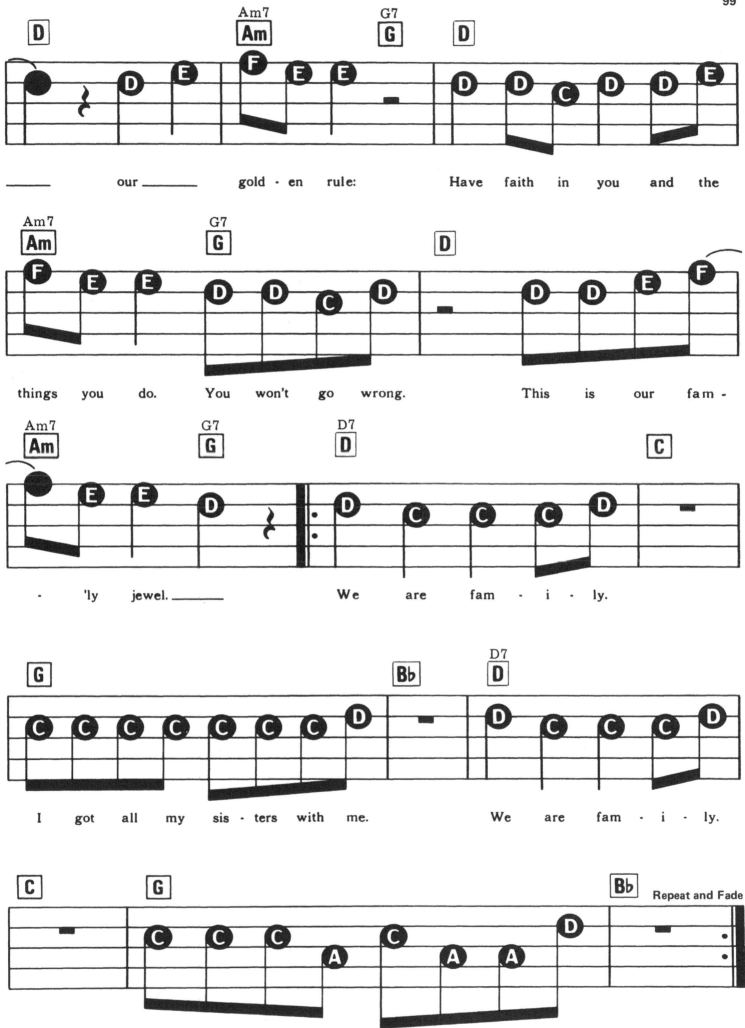

Welcome Back

Words and Music by
John Sebastian

Registration 5
Rhythm: Rock or Disco

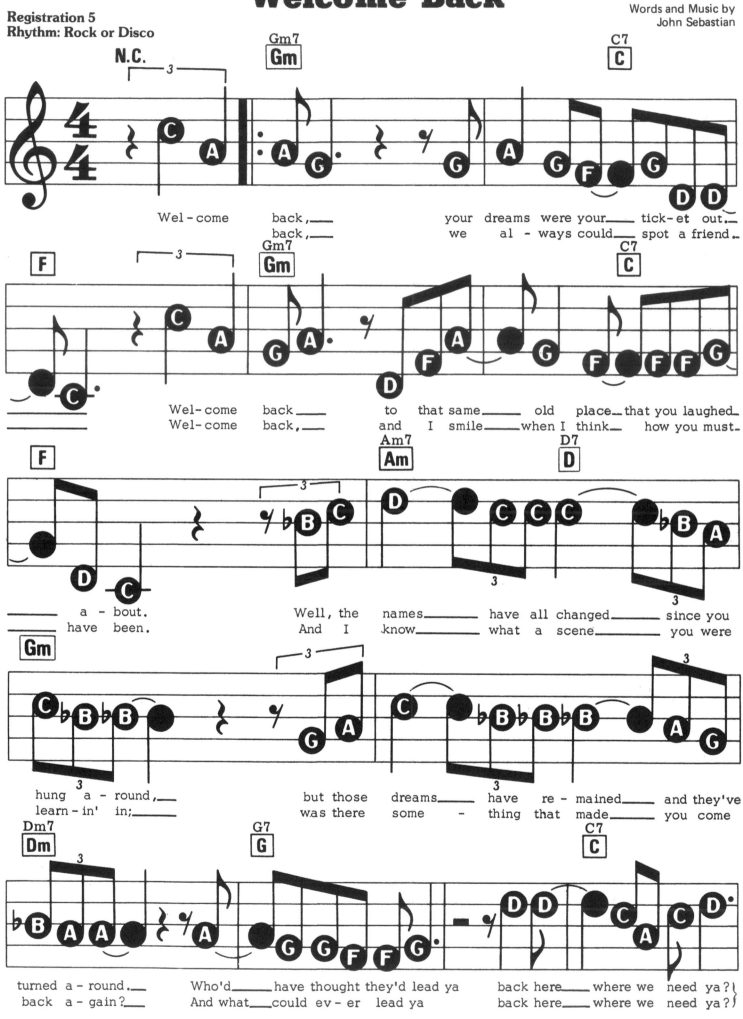

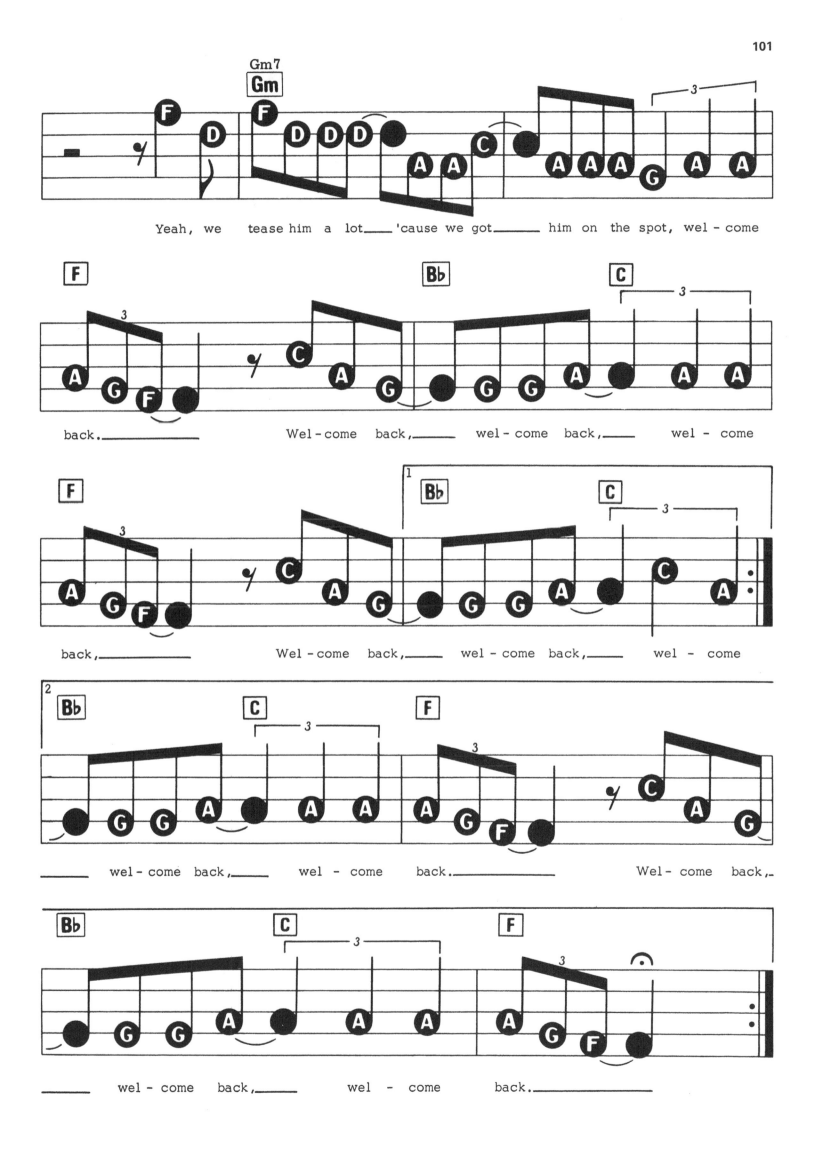

What A Fool Believes

Registration 5
Rhythm: Rock or Disco

Words and Music by Kenny Loggins
and Mike McDonald

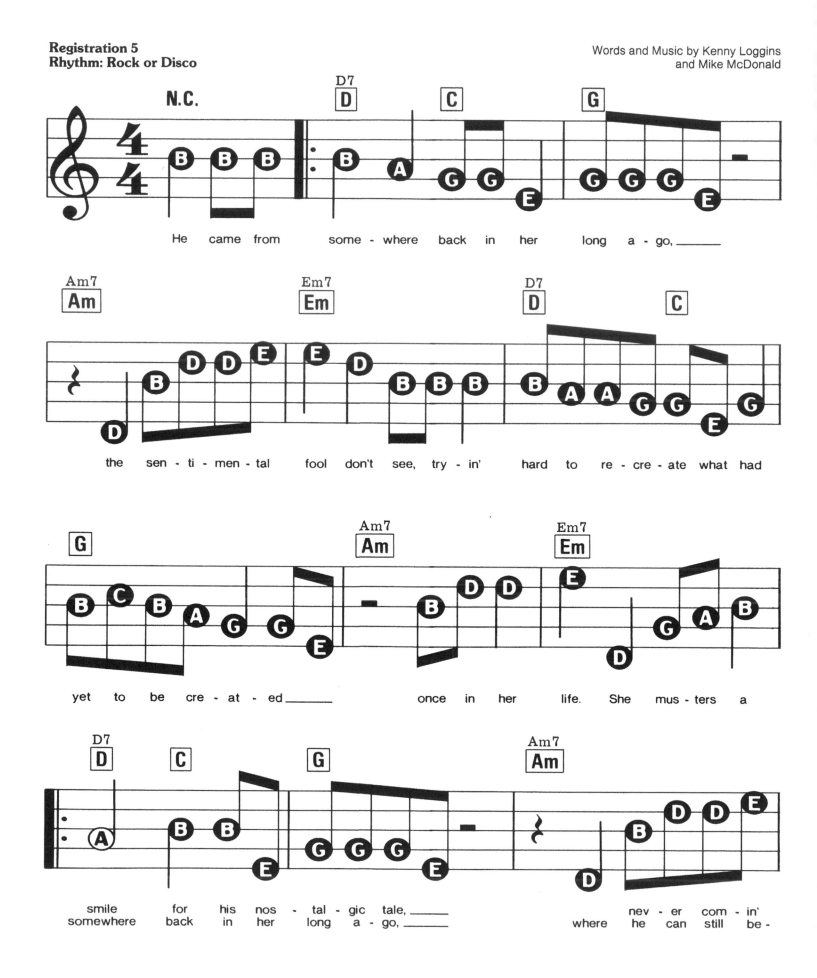

He came from some - where back in her long a - go, _____

the sen - ti - men - tal fool don't see, try - in' hard to re - cre - ate what had

yet to be cre - at - ed _____ once in her life. She mus - ters a

smile for his nos - tal - gic tale, _____
somewhere back in her long a - go, _____
where he can still be-
nev - er com - in'

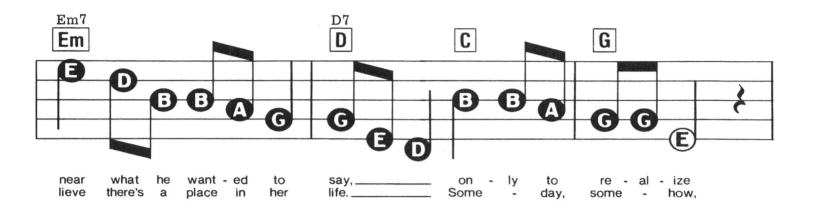

near what he want - ed to say, _____ on - ly to re - al - ize
lieve there's a place in her life. _____ Some - day, some - how,

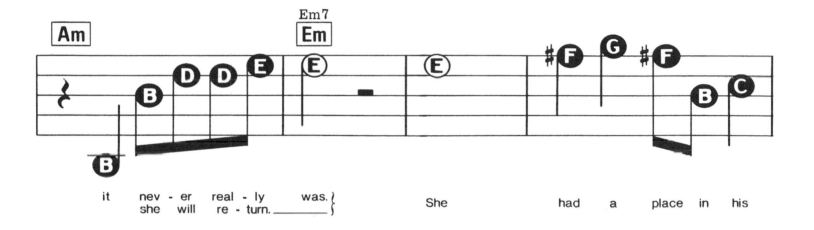

it nev - er real - ly was. } She had a place in his
she will re - turn. _____ }

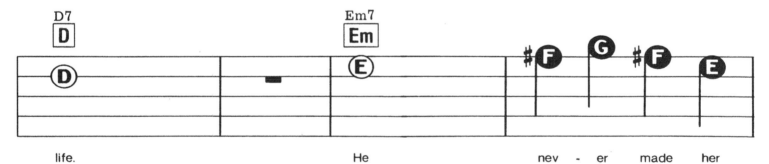

life. He nev - er made her

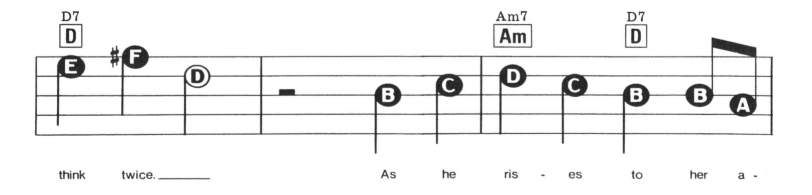

think twice. _____ As he ris - es to her a -

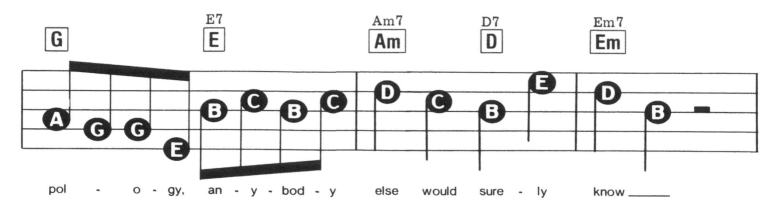

pol - o - gy, an - y - bod - y   else   would   sure - ly   know _____

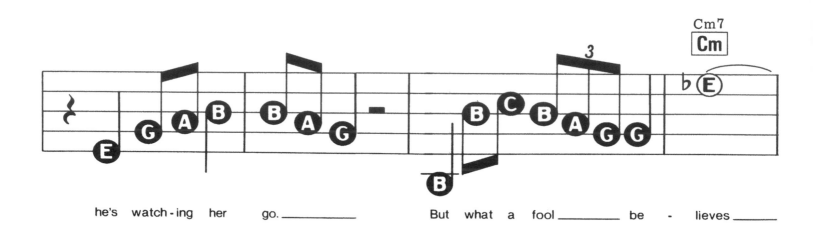

he's   watch - ing   her   go. _____   But   what   a   fool _____   be - lieves _____

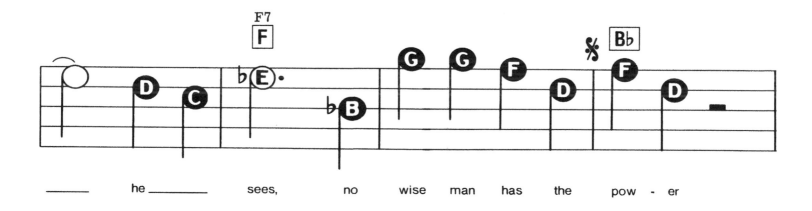

_____   he _____   sees,   no   wise   man   has   the   pow - er

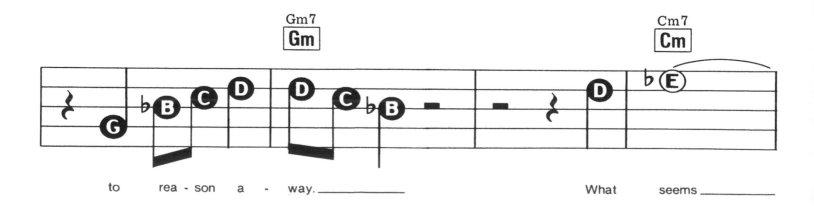

to   rea - son   a - way. _____   What   seems _____

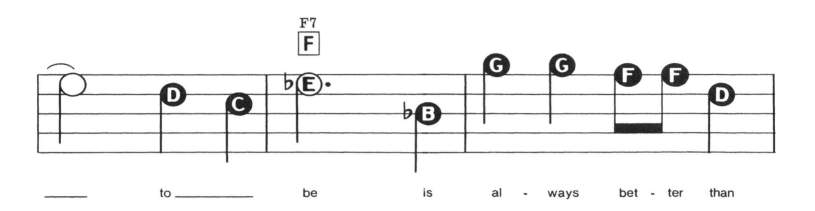

to _____ be is al - ways bet - ter than

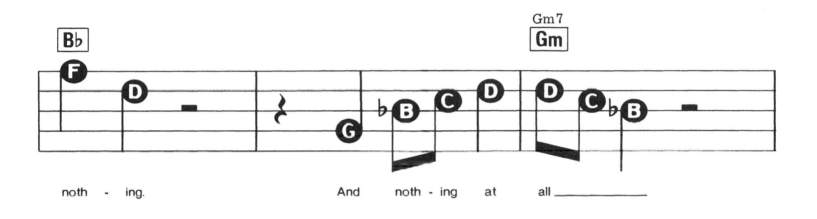

noth - ing. And noth - ing at all _____

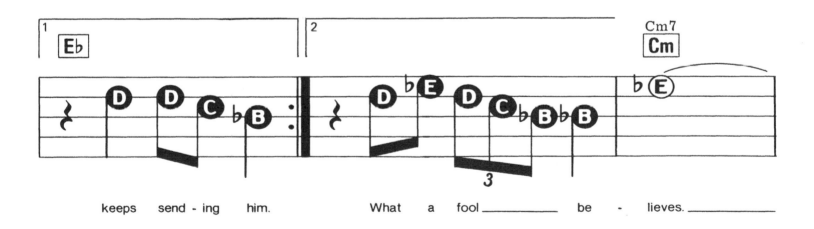

keeps send - ing him. What a fool _____ be - lieves. _____

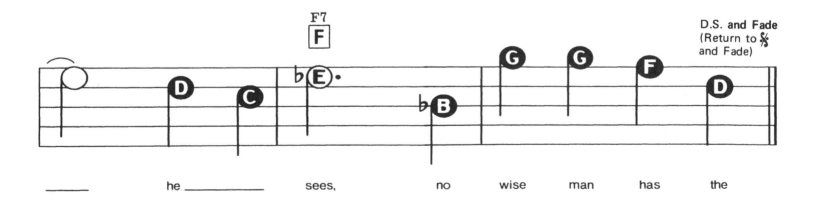

_____ he _____ sees, no wise man has the

The Wreck Of The Edmund Fitzgerald

Words and Music by
Gordon Lightfoot

Registration 2
Rhythm: Waltz

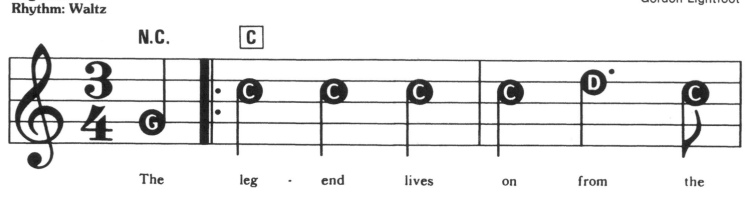

The leg - end lives on from the

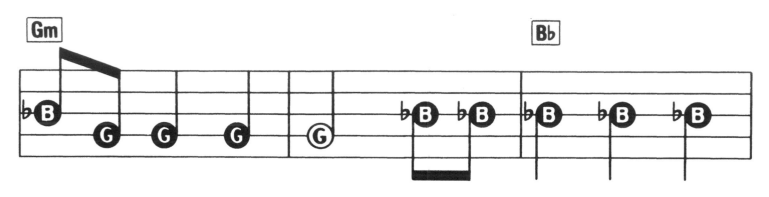

Chip - pe - wa on down of the big lake they

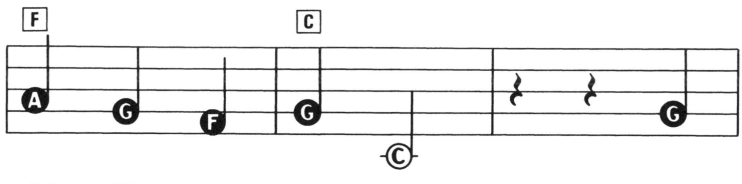

called "Git - che Gu - mee." The

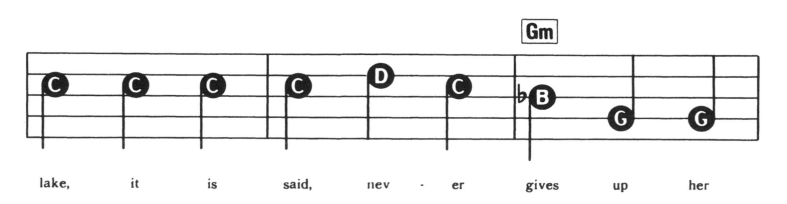

lake, it is said, nev - er gives up her

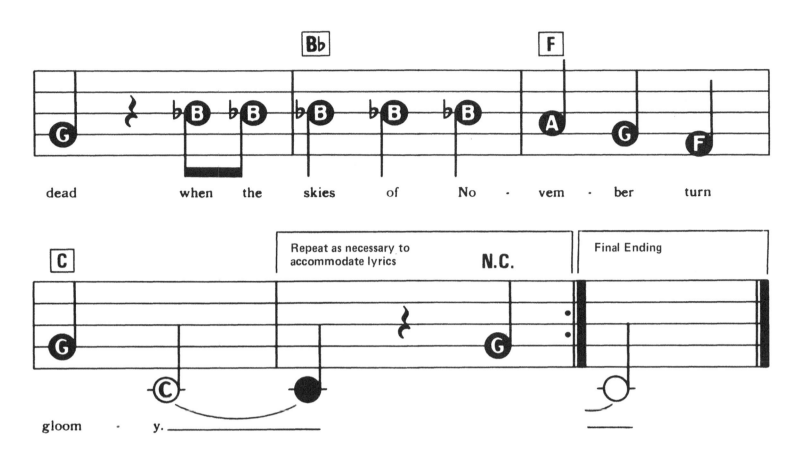

dead   when   the   skies   of   No - vem - ber   turn

Repeat as necessary to accommodate lyrics

N.C.

Final Ending

gloom - y. _____

2. With a load of iron ore twenty-six thousand tons more
   than the Edmund Fitzgerald weighed empty
   that good ship and true was a bone to be chewed
   when the "Gales of November" came early.

3. The ship was the pride of the American side
   coming back from some mill in Wisconsin.
   As the big freighters go it was bigger than most
   with a crew and good captain well seasoned,

4. Concluding some terms with a couple of steel firms
   when they left fully loaded for Cleveland
   And later that night when the ship's bell rang,
   could it be the north wind they'd been feelin'?

5. The wind in the wires made a tattletale sound
   and a wave broke over the railing.
   And ev'ry man knew as the captain did too
   'twas the witch of November come stealin'.

6. The dawn came late and the breakfast had to wait
   when the Gales of November came slashin'.
   When afternoon came it was freezin' rain
   in the face of a hurricane west wind.

7. When suppertime came the old cook came on deck
   sayin', "Fellas, it's too rough t' feed ya."
   At seven P.M. a main hatchway caved in;
   he said "Fellas, it's bin good t' know ya!"

8. The captain wired in he had water comin' in
   and the good ship and crew was in peril.
   And later that night when 'is lights went outta sight
   came the wreck of the Edmund Fitzgerald.

9. Does anyone know where the love of God goes
   when the waves turn the minutes to hours?
   The searchers all say they'd have made Whitefish Bay
   if they'd put fifteen more miles behind 'er.

10. They might have split up or they might have capsized
    they may have broke deep and took water.
    And all that remains is the faces and the names
    of the wives and the sons and the daughters.

11. When Lake Huron rolls, Superior sings
    in the rooms of her ice water mansion.
    Old Michigan steams like a young man's dreams;
    the islands and bays are for sportsmen.

12. And farther below Lake Ontario
    takes in what Lake Erie can send her,
    and the iron boats go as the mariners all know
    with the Gales of November remembered.

13. In a musty old hall in Detroit they prayed,
    in the "Maritime Sailors' Cathedral."
    The church bell chimed 'til it rang twenty-nine times
    for each man of the Edmund Fitzgerald.

14. The legend lives on from the Chippewa on down
    of the big lake they called "Gitche Gumee."
    "Superior," they said, "never gives up her dead
    when the Gales of November come early!"

You Make Lovin' Fun

Registration 5
Rhythm: Rock or Disco

Words and Music by Christine McVie

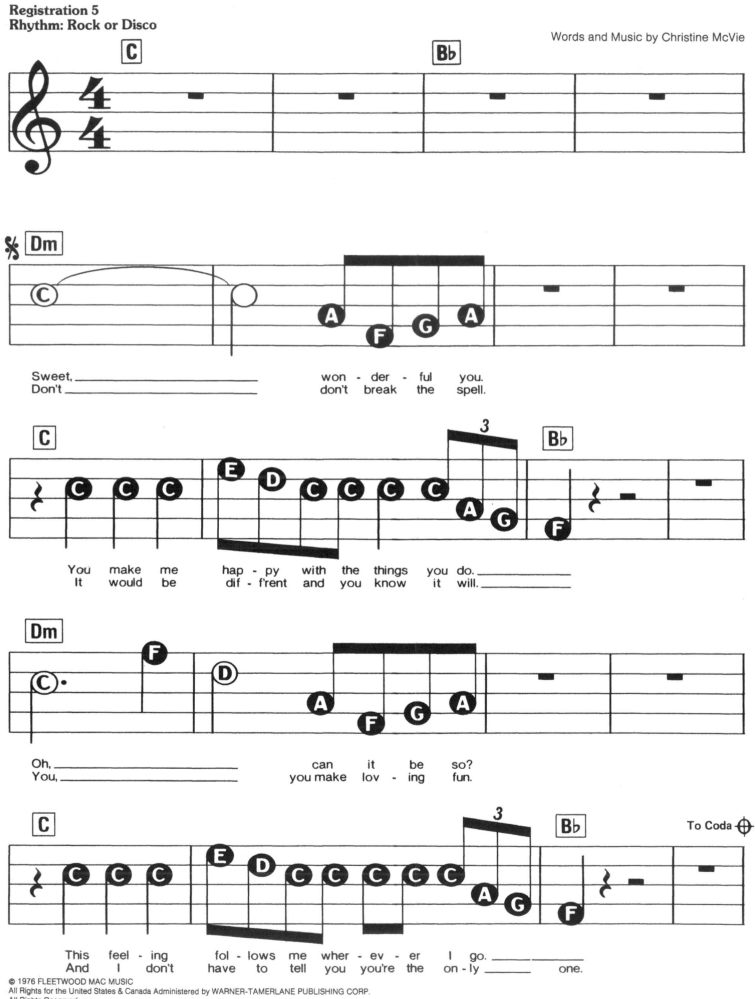

Sweet, _____ won - der - ful you.
Don't _____ don't break the spell.

You make me hap - py with the things you do. _____
It would be dif - f'rent and you know it will. _____

Oh, _____ can it be so?
You, _____ you make lov - ing fun.

This feel - ing fol - lows me wher - ev - er I go. _____
And I don't have to tell you you're the on - ly _____ one.

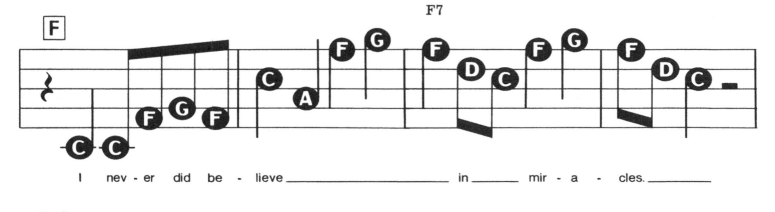

I nev-er did be - lieve _____ in ____ mir - a - cles. _____

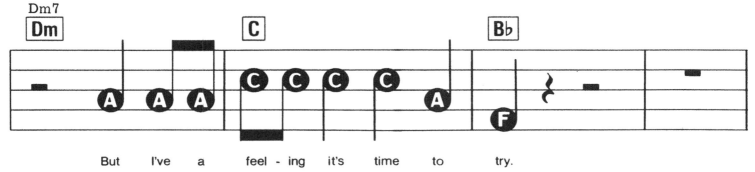

But I've a feel - ing it's time to try.

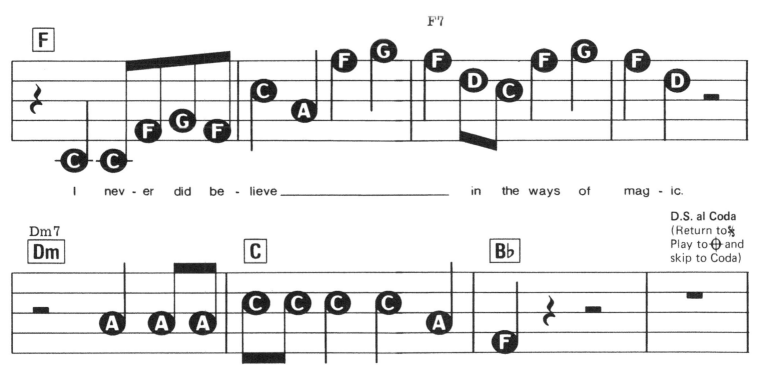

I nev-er did be - lieve _____ in the ways of mag - ic.

D.S. al Coda
(Return to 𝄋
Play to ⊕ and
skip to Coda)

But I'm be - gin - ning to won - der why.

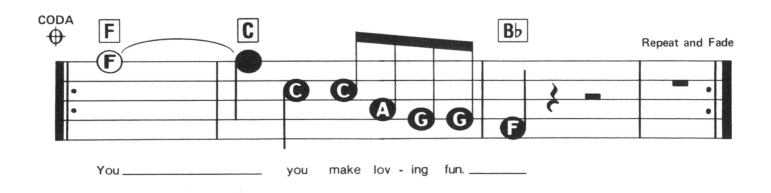

You _____ you make lov - ing fun. _____

Your Mama Don't Dance

Registration 3
Rhythm: Rock or Jazz Rock

By Jim Messina
and Kenny Loggins

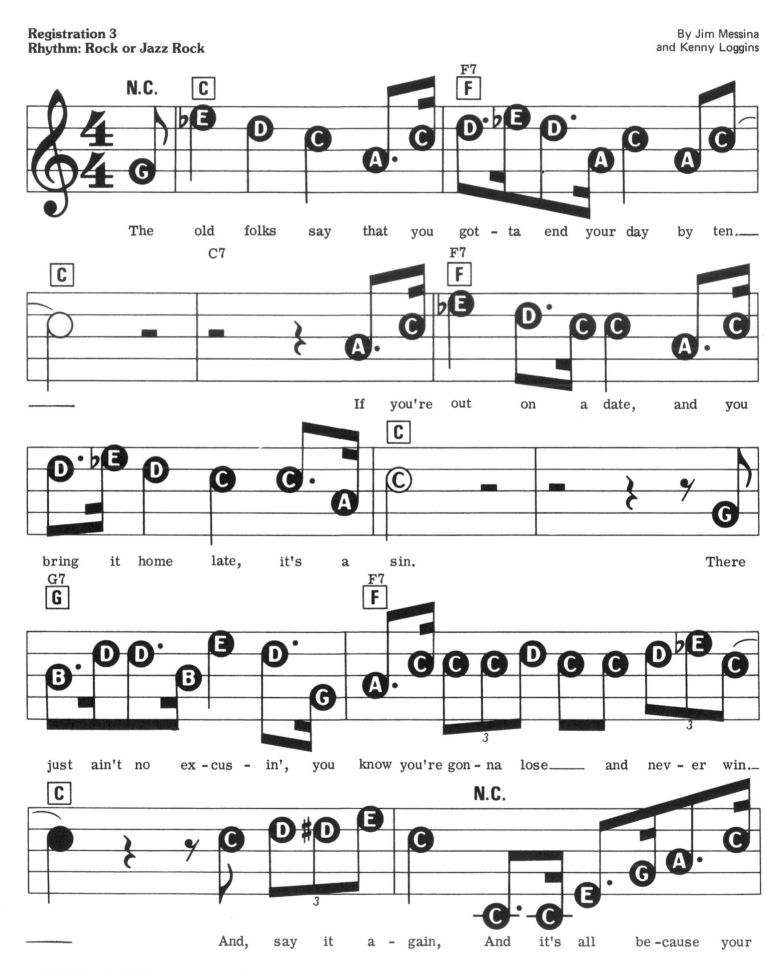

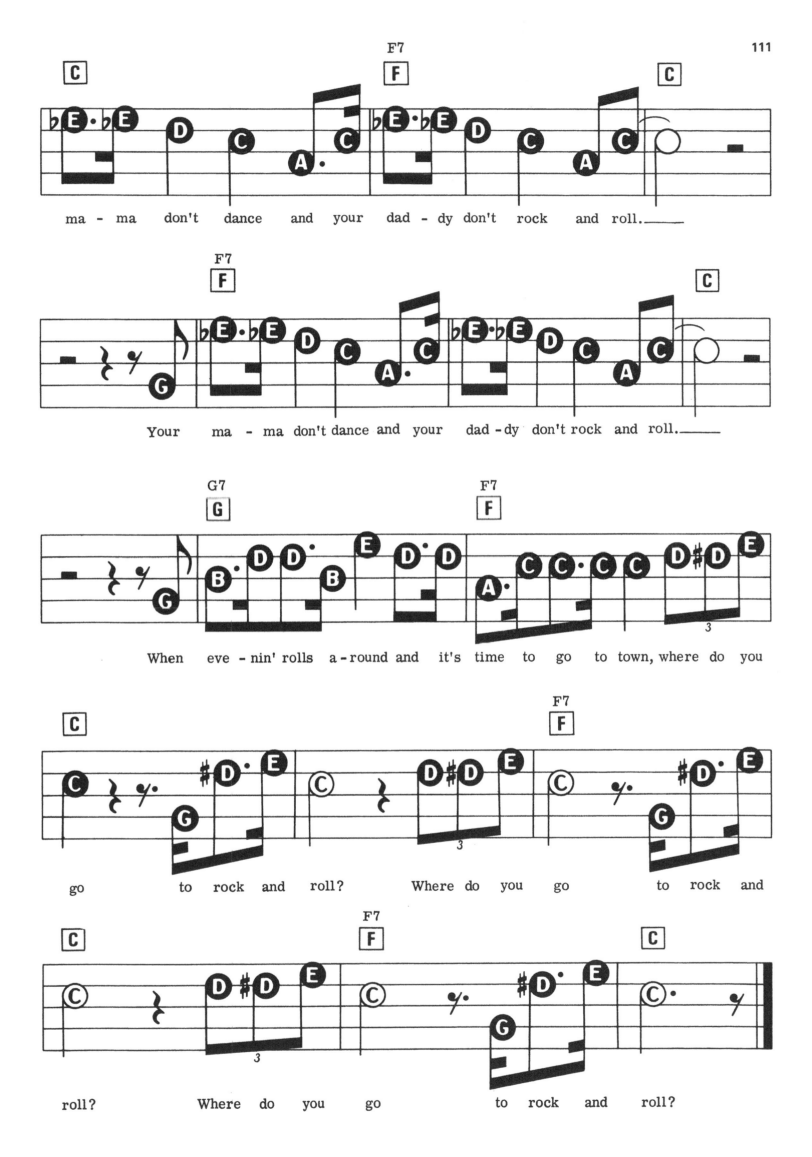

Workin' At The Car Wash Blues

Registration 7
Rhythm: Rock or Jazz Rock

Words and Music by Jim Croce

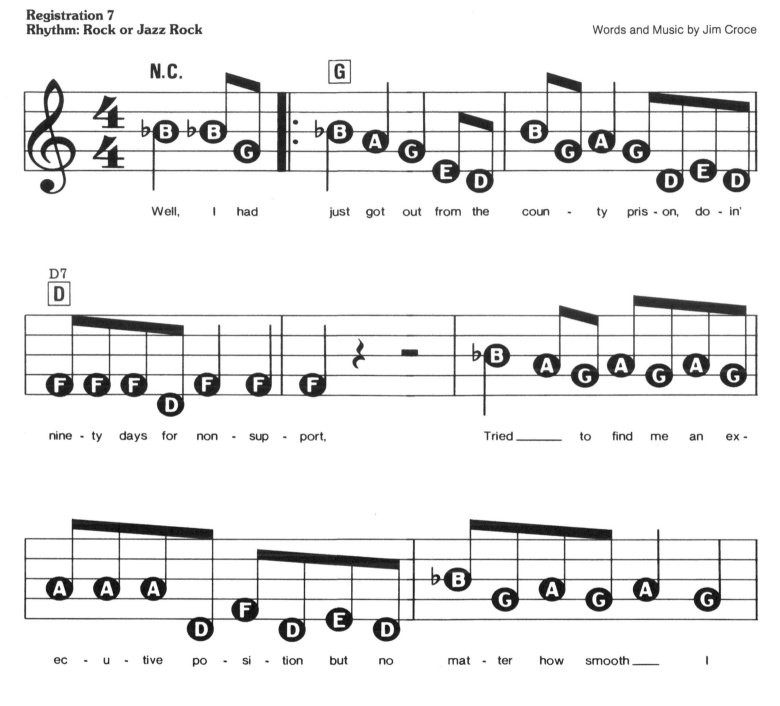

Well, I had just got out from the coun - ty pris - on, do in' nine - ty days for non - sup - port, Tried_____ to find me an ex- ec - u - tive po - si - tion but no mat - ter how smooth_____ I

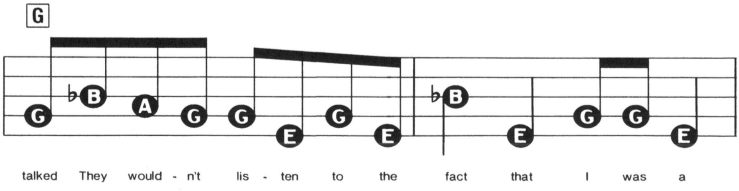

talked They would - n't lis - ten to the fact that I was a

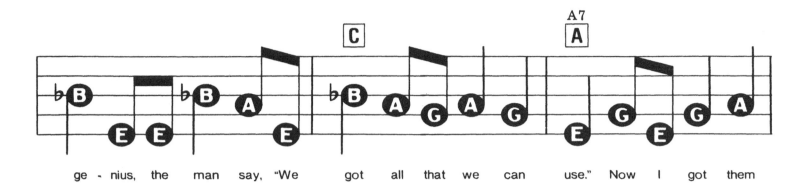

ge - nius, the man say, "We got all that we can use." Now I got them

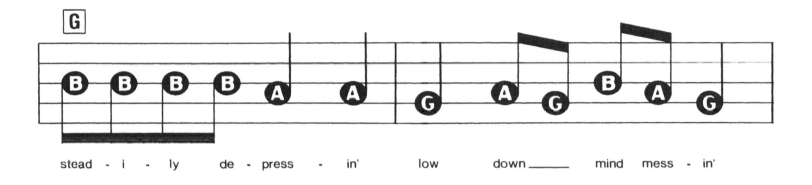

stead - i - ly de - press - in' low down_____ mind mess - in'

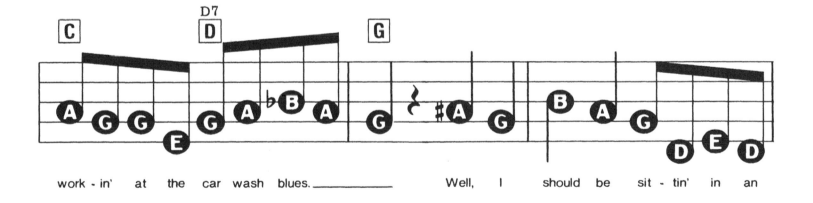

work - in' at the car wash blues._____ Well, I should be sit - tin' in an

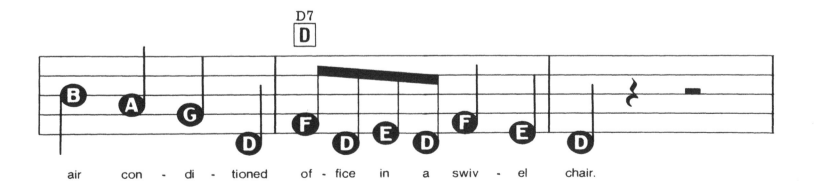

air con - di - tioned of - fice in a swiv - el chair.

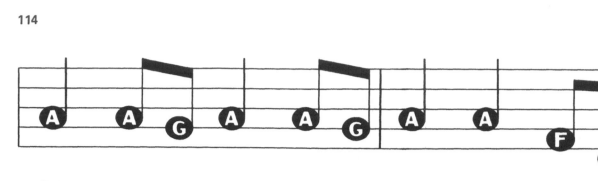

Talk - in' some trash to the sec - re - tar - ies, Say - in',

"Here, now, mom - ma, come on o - ver here." In - stead, I'm stuck here rub - bin' these

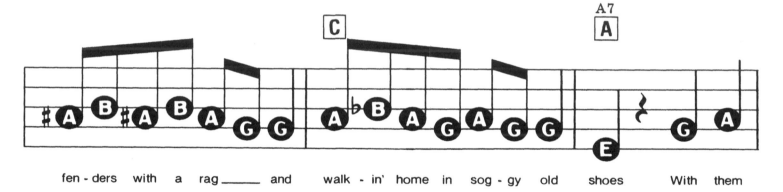

fen - ders with a rag____ and walk - in' home in sog - gy old shoes With them

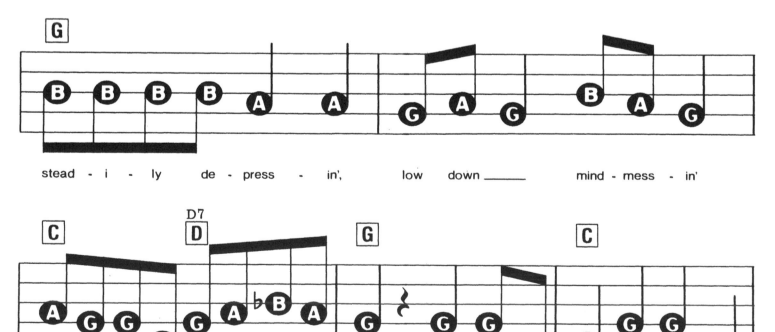

stead - i - ly de - press - in', low down ____ mind - mess - in'

work - in' at the car wash blues._____ You know a man of my a -

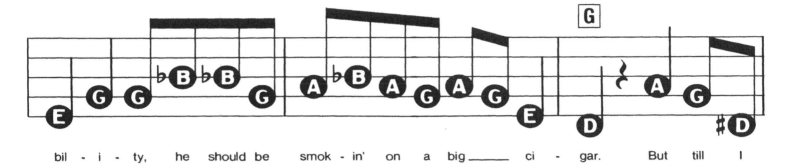

bil - i - ty, he should be smok - in' on a big_____ ci - gar. But till I

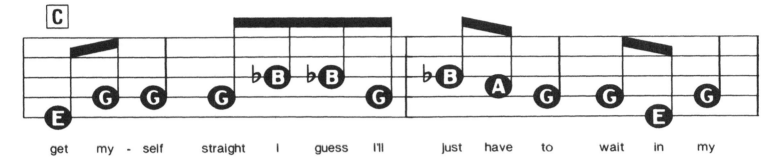

get my - self straight I guess I'll just have to wait in my

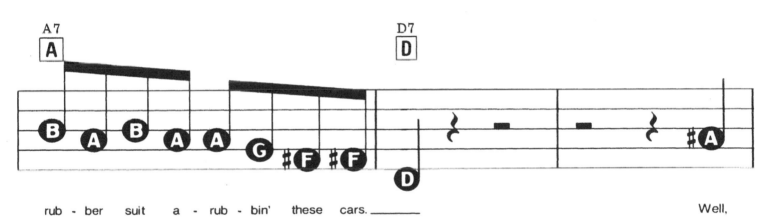

rub - ber suit a - rub - bin' these cars._____ Well,

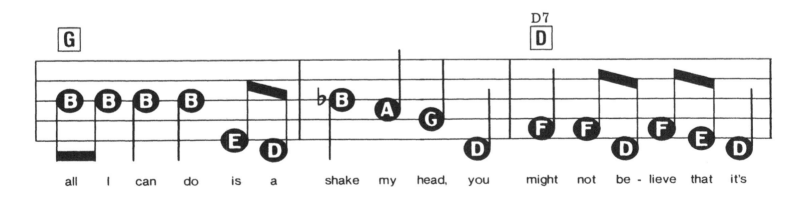

all I can do is a shake my head, you might not be - lieve that it's

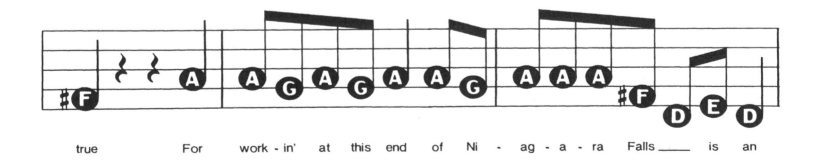

true For work - in' at this end of Ni - ag - a - ra Falls_____ is an

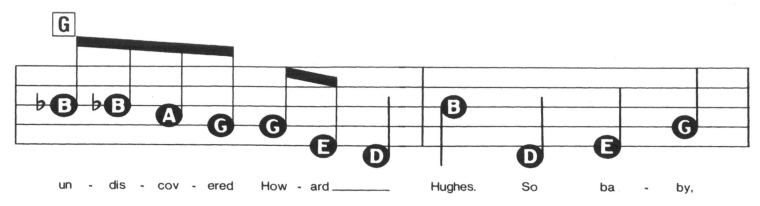

un - dis - cov - ered How - ard _____ Hughes.   So   ba - by,

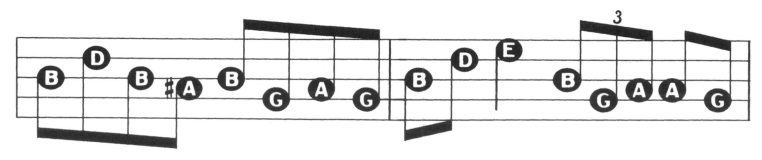

don't ex - pect to see me with no dou - ble mar - ti - ni in an - y

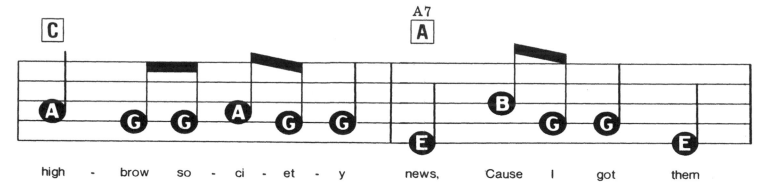

high - brow so - ci - et - y   news,   'Cause   I   got   them

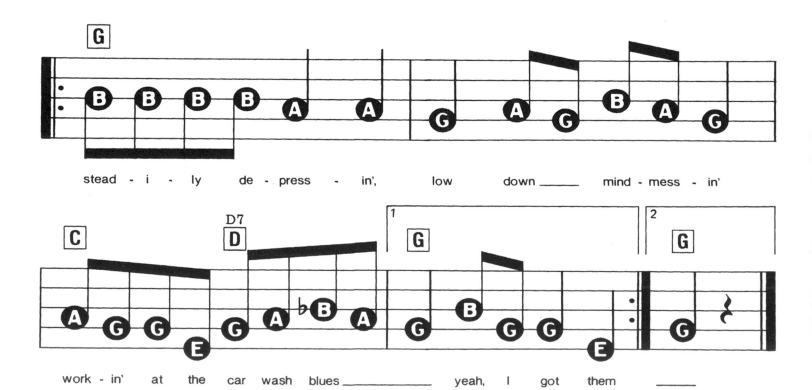

stead - i - ly de - press - in',   low   down _____ mind - mess - in'

work - in' at the car wash blues _____ yeah, I   got   them _____

Chord Speller Chart
of Standard Chord Positions

For those who play standard chord positions, all chords used in the E-Z Play TODAY music arrangements are shown here in their most commonly used chord positions. Suggested fingering is also indicated, but feel free to use alternate fingering.

CHORD FAMILY Abbrev.	MAJOR	MINOR (m)	7TH (7)	MINOR 7TH (m7)
C	5 2 1 G-C-E	5 2 1 G-C-Eb	5 3 2 1 G-Bb-C-E	5 3 2 1 G-Bb-C-Eb
Db	5 2 1 Ab-Db-F	5 2 1 Ab-Db-E	5 3 2 1 Ab-B-Db-F	5 3 2 1 Ab-B-Db-E
D	5 3 1 F#-A-D	5 2 1 A-D-F	5 3 2 1 F#-A-C-D	5 3 2 1 A-C-D-F
Eb	5 3 1 G-Bb-Eb	5 3 1 Gb-Bb-Eb	5 3 2 1 G-Bb-Db-Eb	5 3 2 1 Gb-Bb-Db-Eb
E	5 3 1 G#-B-E	5 3 1 G-B-E	5 3 2 1 G#-B-D-E	5 3 2 1 G-B-D-E
F	4 2 1 A-C-F	4 2 1 Ab-C-F	5 3 2 1 A-C-Eb-F	5 3 2 1 Ab-C-Eb-F
F#	4 2 1 F#-A#-C#	4 2 1 F#-A-C#	5 3 2 1 F#-A#-C#-E	5 3 2 1 F#-A-C#-E
G	5 3 1 G-B-D	5 3 1 G-Bb-D	5 3 2 1 G-B-D-F	5 3 2 1 G-Bb-D-F
Ab	4 2 1 Ab-C-Eb	4 2 1 Ab-B-Eb	5 3 2 1 Ab-C-Eb-Gb	5 3 2 1 Ab-B-Eb-Gb
A	4 2 1 A-C#-E	4 2 1 A-C-E	5 4 2 1 G-A-C#-E	5 4 2 1 G-A-C-E
Bb	4 2 1 Bb-D-F	4 2 1 Bb-Db-F	5 4 2 1 Ab-Bb-D-F	5 4 2 1 Ab-Bb-Db-F
B	5 2 1 F#-B-D#	5 2 1 F#-B-D	5 3 2 1 F#-A-B-D#	5 3 2 1 F#-A-B-D

Guitar Chord Chart

To use the E-Z Play TODAY Guitar Chord chart, simply find the **letter name** of the chord at the top of the chart, and the **kind of chord** (Major, Minor, etc.) in the column at the left. Read down and across to find the correct chord. Suggested fingering has been indicated, but feel free to use alternate fingering.

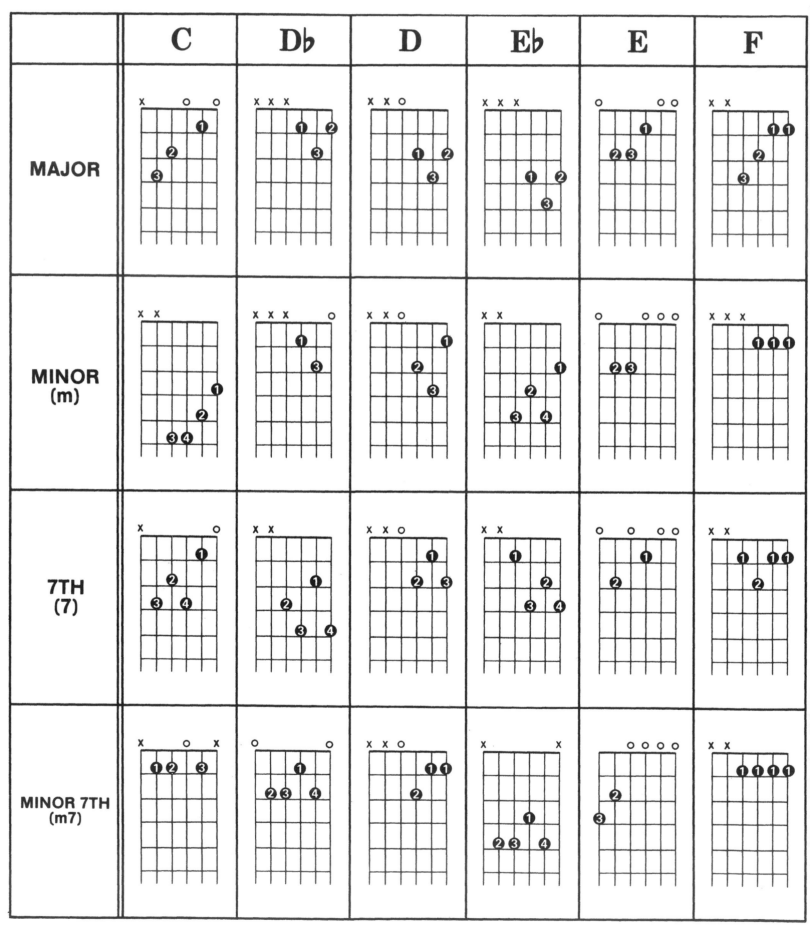

	F♯	G	A♭	A	B♭	B
MAJOR						
MINOR (m)						
7TH (7)						
MINOR 7TH (m7)						

E-Z Play® TODAY Registration Guide For All Organs

On the following chart are 10 numbered registrations for both tonebar (TB) and electronic tab organs. The numbers correspond to the registration numbers on the E-Z Play TODAY songs. Set up as many voices and controls listed for each specific number as you have available on your instrument. For more detailed registrations, ask your dealer for the E-Z Play TODAY Registration Guide for your particular organ model.

REG. NO.		UPPER (SOLO)	LOWER (ACCOMPANIMENT)	PEDAL	GENERALS
1	Tab	Flute 16', 2'	Diapason 8' Flute 4'	Flute 16', 8'	Tremolo/Leslie – Fast
	TB	80 0808 000	(00) 7600 000	46, Sustain	Tremolo/Leslie – Fast (Upper/Lower)
2	Tab	Flute 16', 8', 4', 2', 1'	Diapason 8' Flute 8', 4'	Flute 16' String 8'	Tremolo/Leslie – Fast
	TB	80 7806 004	(00) 7503 000	46, Sustain	Tremolo/Leslie – Fast (Upper/Lower)
3	Tab	Flute 8', 4', 2⅔', 2' String 8', 4'	Diapason 8' Flute 4' String 8'	Flute 16', 8'	Tremolo/Leslie – Fast
	TB	40 4555 554	(00) 7503 333	46, Sustain	Tremolo/Leslie – Fast (Upper/Lower)
4	Tab	Flute 16', 8', 4' Reed 16', 8'	Flute 8', (4) Reed 8'	Flute 8' String 8'	Tremolo/Leslie – Fast
	TB	80 7766 008	(00) 7540 000	54, Sustain	Tremolo/Leslie – Fast (Upper/Lower)
5	Tab	Flute 16', 4', 2' Reed 16', 8' String 8', 4'	Diapason 8' Reed 8' String 4'	Flute 16', 8' String 8'	Tremolo/Leslie
	TB	40 4555 554 Add all 4', 2' voices	(00) 7503 333	57, Sustain	
6	Tab	Flute 16', 8', 4' Diapason 8' String 8'	Diapason 8' Flute 8' String 4'	Diapason 8' Flute 8'	Tremolo/Leslie – Slow (Chorale)
	TB	45 6777 643	(00) 6604 020	64, Sustain	Tremolo/Leslie – Slow (Chorale)
7	Tab	Flute 16', 8', 5⅓', 2⅔', 1'	Flute 8', 4' Reed 8'	Flute 8' String 8'	Chorus (optional) Perc Attack
	TB	88 0088 000	(00) 4333 000	45, Sustain	Tremolo/Leslie – Slow (Chorale)
8	Tab	Piano Preset or Flute 8' or Diapason 8'	Diapason 8'	Flute 8'	
	TB	00 8421 000	(00) 4302 010	43, Sustain	Perc Piano
9	Tab	Clarinet Preset or Flute 8' Reed 16', 8'	Flute 8' Reed 8'	Flute 16', 8'	Vibrato
	TB	00 8080 840	(00) 5442 000	43, Sustain	Vibrato
10	Tab	String (Violin) Preset or Flute 16' String 8', 4'	Flute 8' Reed 8'	Flute 16', 8'	Vibrato or Delayed Vibrato
	TB	00 7888 888	(00) 7765 443	57, Sustain	Vibrato or Delayed Vibrato

NOTE: TIBIAS may be used in place of FLUTES.
VIBRATO may be used in place of LESLIE.